BASIC PRINCIPLES OF AIR WARFARE

(THE INFLUENCE OF AIR POWER ON SEA AND LAND STRATEGY)

By
SQUADRON - LEADER

ALDERSHOT :
GALE & POLDEN, Ltd., WELLINGTON WORKS.
ALSO AT LONDON AND PORTSMOUTH.
1927

Price - SEVEN SHILLINGS & SIXPENCE *Nett.*

Dedicated

TO THE MEMORY OF
LIEUTENANT B. CARLETON-SMITH

(OBSERVER, NO. 100 SQUADRON, ROYAL AIR FORCE)

———o———

"If more depends on the pilot, it is equally true to say that a higher degree of cold-drawn courage is demanded from the observer. . . . There is no more splendid record of service in the war than the record of the best observers. . . . The single wing of the observer's badge was the mark of service done over the fire of enemy guns."—Raleigh ("War in the Air," Vol. I).

FOREWORD

BY

MAJOR-GENERAL SIR EDMUND IRONSIDE, K.C.B., C.M.G., D.S.O.

SUCCESS in war will go to that nation which best knows how to economize its man-power through the use of modern weapons. No single weapon of war alone, no matter how powerful, is sufficient in itself to effect the purpose of war—the defeat of the enemy. Only the closest co-operation between the forces operating the different weapons can bring about the desired result, and for proper co-operation one must have knowledge. The author has given us a reasoned explanation of the task which lies before the Royal Air Force. He is to be congratulated upon having given the military world a basis from which can be built a proper system of co-operation between the Air and the Navy and Army.

Ironside
M.G.

CONTENTS

A RETROSPECT ix

CHAPTER. PAGE

I.—INTRODUCTORY 1

II.—(1) AIR SUPERIORITY 11
    (2) AIR COMBAT AND SUPERIORITY OF MORAL 17
    (3) IMPORTANCE OF PRODUCTION AND RESERVES 20

III.—(1) OFFENCE AND DEFENCE 27
    (2) PRINCIPLE OF CONCENTRATION 36
    (3) PRINCIPLE OF SURPRISE 44
    (4) PRINCIPLE OF ECONOMY OF FORCE ... 46
    (5) MAINTENANCE OF THE OBJECT 47
    (6) DIVERSIONS 52

IV.—THE PRINCIPAL OBJECTIVE OF AIR FORCES 54
    INTRODUCTORY TO COMBINED OPERATIONS: CO-OPERATION 71

V.—THE INFLUENCE OF AIR POWER ON SEA WARFARE 73

VI—THE INFLUENCE OF AIR POWER ON LAND WARFARE 94

VII.—CONCLUSIONS 114

APPENDICES 135

A RETROSPECT

In the year A.D. 1903, in a certain island known as Great Britain, there existed two armed Forces of the Crown—a Navy and an Army—the one to fight at sea, the other on land.

In the same year, there arose two pioneers known as the Wright brothers, which two adventurous men, after long, costly and diligent experiment and research within their own country, invented a machine in which they achieved a miracle: for, behold, they did fly in the air.

And in due time the invention was demonstrated before high officials of the aforesaid armed forces, who at the beginning regarded the flying machine as a plaything, failing to appreciate its potentialities as a future weapon of war.

Thereafter, the amazing development of the invention moved them to devote to it much thought. Neither body took counsel with the other as to the best methods of perfecting the machine. Instead, each went to work in its own way, forming two branches comprising aircraft units, the one known as the Royal Naval Air Service, the other as the Royal Flying Corps. Each regarded the invention as an interesting novelty, and neither would co-operate with the other concerning it.

And it came to pass that in the year A.D. 1914 their country became engaged in a war which lasted many years, during which the two flying services grew rapidly and the importance of the discovery increased to dimensions undreamed of. So that men marvelled and the civilian population became exceedingly concerned and perturbed.

And they cried out for protection, perceiving that the flying machines were able to bring war to their very doors, being able to evade the sea and land defences.

Now, between the two flying services there existed no co-ordination, with the result that the most effective use was not made of the material, while economy of force was relegated to the background. The respective duties and functions of the two arms were not defined, nor could they be, for responsibility was divided within their councils. Concentration of effort, without which success could not be achieved, was made impossible.

In the year A.D. 1918, there arose great consternation in the land, and a few wise men, realizing that divided effort could not be permitted to continue with impunity, held a council of war, and decided that the two flying services should be amalgamated. His Majesty the King approved their action and consented to the formation of one air arm, to be known as the Royal Air Force. In due course, the war was won, and the new Force was set the task of consolidating its position and of laying a solid foundation in peace upon which the future security of the country and its Empire could rest.

And, in spite of enormous difficulties, the Air Force of the country firmly established itself foremost in efficiency amongst the nations of the world. The spirit of co-operation was once more manifest, and the three Imperial Forces worked together in perfect amity.

There is one law of the sea, one of the land, and another of the air, but common to all three there are principles of war which change only in their application. These are eight in number.

    1. Maintenance of the Object.
    2. Offensive action.
    3. Surprise.
    4. Concentration.

A RETROSPECT

5. Economy of Force.
6. Security.
7. Mobility.
8. CO-OPERATION.

Each is the complement of the remainder. The one most frequently disregarded is the last—perhaps not because it *is* last (and there is, indeed, no reason why it should not be first)—but because the conquest of human nature is one of the most difficult of the many difficult tasks confronting mankind.

BOOKS CONSULTED

"The Direction of War." Major-General Sir W. D. Bird.
"The Reformation of War." Col. J. F. C. Fuller.
"Precepts and Judgments." Marshal Foch.
"War in the Air," Vol. I. Sir Walter Raleigh.
"Air Power and War Rights." Spaight.
"Imperial Military Geography." Cole.
"The Problem of Defence." Sir George Aston.
Naval and Military Despatches relating to the Great War, 1914-18.
"From Private to Field-Marshal." Field-Marshal Sir William Robertson.
Field Service Regulations, Vol. II (Operations), 1920.
"The Dover Patrol," Vols. I and II. Admiral Sir Reginald Bacon.
"Naval Operations," Vols. I-III. Sir Julian Corbett.
"Some Principles of Maritime Strategy." Corbett.
"Twenty-five Years." Earl Grey of Fallodon.
"The Crisis of the Naval War." Admiral Viscount Jellicoe.
"The World Crisis." Rt. Hon. Winston Churchill.
"Soldiers and Statesmen," Vols. I and II. Field-Marshal Sir William Robertson.
"Governments and War." General Sir F. Maurice.

BASIC PRINCIPLES OF AIR WARFARE

CHAPTER I.

INTRODUCTORY.

DURING the eight years that have passed since the war of 1914-1918, much thought has been directed to the question of the air defence of this country. In the same period, important strides have been made in the development of aircraft.

Meanwhile, there has grown up throughout Central Europe a network of air lines which is being extended rapidly. If the rate of progress continues—and all the signs indicate a substantial acceleration—there will be few countries which cannot be reached by air. Within the space of a few years, a new era of travel has been introduced. Its importance in relation to the problems affecting the security and prosperity of the British Empire needs no emphasis. The defence of our worldwide communications will become even more complicated. On the other hand, the value to the Empire of a more rapid means of communication and of a more *mobile defence* cannot as yet be fully assessed.

In future wars, aircraft must play a part no less important than naval forces. Essential as it is that we shall possess as of old a Navy second to none for the control of sea communications, yet it cannot be doubted that the influence of sea power will, under the new conditions, not only be modified, but will depend to an ever-increasing degree on the support of the air arm.

The author does not accept the belief that the forces of the air will supplant those of the sea and the land. He prefers to regard all three services as essentially complementary. That air forces, however efficient and brilliantly directed, will be able to control sea communications or to win battles on land, is a figment which needs little refutation. Progress in the use and development of a new weapon of war is necessarily slow, and its evolution may be equally retarded by enthusiastic advocacy and avowed scepticism.

It is the author's intention, from a study of the late war, to place on record certain incidents and to deduce therefrom what he conceives to be sound principles in regard to the employment of air forces in possible future campaigns. In a volume such as this, attempting to deal with highly-controversial problems, much of the contents must consist of excerpts. The author is hopeful, at least, that this book will serve the purpose of promoting a better conception of the principles which govern air warfare generally.

Doctrines of the conduct of war have been influenced from time to time in various directions, largely because of the fact that yesterday one new element, to-day another new element, assumes preponderating importance.

In the latest phase, the use of the air, it would seem that we have not arrived at a clear and uniform point of view. It does not appear that we have yet drawn, in any precise measure, sound conclusions from the experiences of modern war, particularly the warfare of the air. We are dominated too largely, I think, by some specially striking incidents, attributing to them an importance which closer examination proves to be exaggerated.

Beyond question there is a great need of study, not only in regard to a comprehensive doctrine of air warfare generally, but also as to the effect, strategical and tactical, which the new arm has had already on the application of the principles governing the conduct of war on sea and on land. To dogmatize about the employment of aircraft in war is futile, inasmuch as we have comparatively little historical guidance to rely upon. I suggest, nevertheless, that the experiences gained during the war of 1914-18 are adequate for the deduction of sound general principles. By examining the data available, by reviewing war in all its phases, and by avoiding mere speculation, conclusions may be deduced which will lead to a better understanding of the whole problem.

Corbett's dictum on the study of history is one that should be taken to heart. " Officers," he wrote, " no longer look upon History as a kind of dust heap. . . . They go to it as a mine of experience where alone the gold is to be found, *from which right doctrine—the soul of war—can be built up.*" To become distinguished, one must read, for without it abilities are of little use. In order to prepare oneself for the higher posts, constant study is necessary. This should be done from the very commencement of one's service career, for in later years when a position of responsibility is reached far less time is at our disposal in which to study.

There is only one method of fitting our intellects to be ready for war; and that is by studying the history of air warfare, *and by no means should we neglect naval and land warfare.*

The more we study the art of war in all its elements, and the more fully all three services are alive to what is essential in war generally, and in the conduct of modern warfare particularly, the more uniform and efficient will be the co-operation of every branch of the Navy, Army and Air Force. The task of the future will only be solved if, in the words of Field-Marshal Earl Haig, "we have an intelligent understanding of the other man's job."

I shall endeavour to develop principles of air warfare that are of general application. The characteristic features of all warfare depend upon them, and I will try to say only that which is absolutely necessary in regard to them and to avoid entering into any theoretical discourse.

Primarily, let us study the restrictions imposed upon aircraft.

Firstly, we find in practice that in air warfare, as in all warfare, the enemy is armed similarly to ourselves. This is also true of anti-aircraft defence. It is true that such defences have not proved a very effective means of destroying aircraft; nevertheless, they act as a deterrent and impose upon aircraft definite restrictions.

Secondly, we will consider the limitations imposed by the weather. This difficulty does not seem to be insuperable, and it is claimed that with the progress of science it will be possible ultimately for aircraft to operate successfully whatever the meteorological conditions. Nevertheless, although aircraft may be able to keep in the air under very adverse weather conditions, I think it must be admitted, at any rate for the time being, that such conditions will restrict the operations of aircraft in war. On the other hand, certain conditions of weather may, for example, assist attacking aircraft and render both aircraft in defence and the anti-aircraft ground defences ineffective.

Thirdly, the greater the power of offence that is given an aeroplane, the less power of self-defence it will have and the lower the altitude it will be able to reach. This is precisely the opposite to the case of the warship, in which any increase in offensive power leads to an increase in its capacity for defence. But here again we must not imagine that the offensive powers of aircraft cannot be increased to any appreciable extent. There is little doubt that with the advance of aeronautical science this present defect will in time be considerably lessened. We have only to examine the advancement made during the past few years to see that much has been accomplished in this direction.

The cycle in the development of any new weapon is, as a rule, sufficiently outlined to enable us to make certain important deductions, but as to this point it is well to remember that the aeroplane is a new arm that moves in an element, the air, which is denied to the weapons of the sea and land forces. Therefore, we cannot approach this question from the same relative angle as when dealing with new and improved weapons designed for use in sea or land warfare.

Fourthly, restriction is placed upon the action of aircraft on account of their inability to maintain a continuous bombardment. This is said to be their chief limitation. It may be claimed justly that the moral effect of an air bombardment is far greater than anything to which we have been accustomed hitherto, and therefore a continuous bombardment is not necessary to achieve the object in view. What is, I think, of greater importance is the fact that aircraft, with their immense speed and radius of action, possess offensive qualities incomparably greater than those of any other arm.

It must, however, be realized that armed conflict between opposing air forces is becoming more extensive. It follows that to attain their object, the carrying out of an effective bombardment, aircraft will have to fight the opposing aircraft or evade them. Will evasion be possible? I will leave this point for future discussion. Let those who imagine that victory will be attained by attacks on the civil population not be misled into the belief that this form of attack is possible without battle.

There is a further important aspect which concerns us as an island Power. It is this: that, so long as we possess both sea and air power, we shall be able to carry war into the enemy's country and fight our battles abroad as hitherto. Occupation requires land forces; these, in our case at least, need sea power to permit of their concentration and supply. Armies and fleets must each have their proportion of aircraft to enable them to fulfil their own functions, and we need an air force to strike *in conjunction with* the sea or land forces. In short, we cannot employ an army without sea or air power. Sea and air power are, moreover, essential to secure the ocean transport by which we live and to protect our own land from air attacks.

It is to be hoped that we shall hear no more about one fighting service being of supreme importance and the others of little or none. We must maintain a navy second to none. Land fighting occurs in all great wars and therefore land forces are necessary. Again, neither the Navy nor the Army can fight effectively without the assistance of the Air Force. Each service is, as I have already said, the complement of the other two.

It is time, I think, we dropped the rather loose term " Independent " applied, apparently, to that part of the Air Force that is not directly operating with naval or military forces. Marshal Foch hits the nail on the head when he says :—

"Those words, *common action, union of forces,* mean the reverse of independent, isolated, or successive action, which would lead fatally to dispersion. It is obvious, therefore, *that any one of the units which is a component part of the whole force* is not free to act on its own account, to seek the enemy and fight him *where* and *when* it likes." *No action in war on the part of any portion of the armed forces can be termed independent.* Apart from this more important aspect of the question, it is a term which is undesirable, for it is at variance with the principle of co-operation in war. Let us at least be careful how and when we use this term, if at all. All arms are inter-dependent, as also are the various types of aircraft.

Both naval and air forces are equally vital to our existence as an island Power, and so to the British Empire as a whole. Our air forces must be equal to the tasks of defending our interests throughout the British Empire and of attacking those air forces that may threaten any part of it. The defeat of our air forces would bring incalculable results in its train and would in certain circumstances render our Navy and Army powerless to act. This necessitates our maintaining sufficiently strong air forces, so situated strategically, that they are able to secure all points vital to our existence. The distribution of our air forces must be designed to this end. Undue dispersion must be avoided. Above all, we must remember that it is only by the co-operation of all arms that success is attained.

Let us not be beguiled into employing our forces on missions that can have little or no effect on the main issues of the war. Nor must circumstances deflect us from the purpose which we have set out to achieve. We must have at all times a clear understanding of what our object is and should then concentrate our whole efforts upon attaining that object. Half-hearted measures never succeed, and every endeavour must be made to avoid failure and the whittling away of any force, however small it may be. If definite results cannot be achieved, it is worse than useless to make the attempt, for such action can only lead to furthering the enemy's aims and playing into his hands. Whatever the task, we must ensure that it is within our powers of achievement and that the forces we employ are sufficient for success. In this respect we should do our utmost to utilize to the best purpose the lives of those entrusted to our keeping, and avoid their sacrifice in a vain endeavour to achieve something that is of small importance and not strictly essential to the fulfilment of our country's aims. In the excitement and strain of war, this is often forgotten.

It is a trite but true saying that in peace we must prepare ourselves for war. War is an art, in which no man may reach perfection, however much practice or study be devoted to it. Yet only by study can we dare hope to succeed.

The real object of war is "to break the will of the enemy *in such a way* as to make him conform to our policy." This, doubtless, has caused many to jump to the conclusion that aircraft, because of their ability to strike directly at the enemy people, are the readiest means by which this can be attained, ignoring the fact that defeat of the enemy's air forces is an essential preliminary. The fundamental idea of all warfare may be expressed in the postulate, "To use the forces available *in such a way* as to secure, in case of success, the most decisive effect imaginable—in other words, to shake or break the will of the enemy in the surest manner."

The whole crux of the matter lies *in the method* by which this is assured. By what method can the enemy be defeated in the surest and quickest manner? It is clear in itself that a truly decisive result can only be assured in the first instance by the defeat of his organized forces. This alone is the real determining issue.

The argument that "The influence of air power on the ability of one nation to impress its will on another in armed contest will be decisive," is one to which much prominence has been given. I shall deal with this point in greater detail in a later chapter. It is an arguable question whether a sustained effort will succeed and whether sufficient strength can be found for such effort. Taking all the elements into consideration, I think not, for one reason to which allusion may here be made.

This new weapon, with its long radius of action, both for offence and defence, is subject to the same psychological rules that govern all armament. Armament begets armament. The late war proved this to be equally true of aircraft, and the future will show more and more that success in war, whatever the type of craft employed, can only be achieved by fighting.

The use of new weapons will not necessarily change the ultimate character of war. The next war may start in the air—it will not end there. The truth of this depends, however, on the character of the conflict. I think it is true to say that, so long as the armed forces are undefeated, the security of the nation and its interests will be assured. It may be argued that we came within measurable distance of defeat by the submarine, and that it is therefore feasible to win a war by economic pressure or by moral attacks on the civilian population. Economic pressure and attacks against moral are purely a means to an end; they may, indeed, have a very great influence upon the winning or losing of a war, but the ultimate result will depend upon whether *the armed forces are defeated.* Economic pressure and attacks against moral may, indeed, assist in the defeat of a nation and its armed forces, but the *surest and quickest* method of winning a war is to defeat the armed forces of the enemy.

A weapon of the future and one that may have far-reaching consequences is gas, employed either in the form of a gas bomb or spray. If the development of this weapon, more especially in the latter form, should make possible its extensive employment by aircraft, the effect upon future warfare would be enormous. I shall not enter here into a technical or detailed discussion on the point, for there are reasons which would make that course undesirable. It is, however, a subject to which attention must be given by those responsible for the country's security. It is essential not only that we are prepared to meet any such attack and to minimize its effect, but also, so long as such a form of warfare is possible, to ensure that we ourselves are equipped with similar and even more efficient means to be employed against an unscrupulous foe.

Finally, it cannot be emphasized too strongly that complete preparations to meet air attacks must be made during peace, for time will not permit of any improvization of air defences on the outbreak of war.

Marshal Foch is quoted as saying : " Every military operation must be approached from the side of its object, in the widest sense of that word, What is the Problem ? Everything in war is linked together, is mutually inter-dependent, mutually inter-penetrating. Each operation has a *raison d'être,* that is, an object; that object, once determined, fixes the nature and the value of the means to be employed as well as the use which ought to be made of the forces."

To defeat the enemy's air forces in order to gain " air superiority "; to adopt, with this primary end in view, the methods and tactics which may lead to it in the quickest and surest manner, is the primary object of air warfare. The destruction of the enemy's air forces, in the air and at their bases, is the most effective method of attaining it. To this end must be subjected all other operations until, at least, air superiority has been attained.

CHAPTER II.

(1) AIR SUPERIORITY.

(2) AIR COMBAT AND SUPERIORITY OF MORAL.

(3) IMPORTANCE OF PRODUCTION AND RESERVES.

BEFORE it is possible to discuss particular forms of air warfare or the principles which govern it, it is necessary first of all to deal with that branch of the subject which has for the want of a better term been termed "Air Superiority." This undoubtedly forms the foundation upon which we must build.

In 1911 the Committee of Imperial Defence appointed a technical sub-committee to give advice on the measures which should be taken to secure for the country an efficient air service. In a memorandum submitted to this sub-committee by Capt. Bertram Dickson the following passage appears : " In case of a European war between two countries, both sides would be equipped with large corps of aeroplanes, each trying to obtain information of the other, and to hide its own movements. The efforts which each would exert in order to hinder or prevent the enemy from obtaining information . . . would lead to the inevitable result of a war in the air, for the supremacy of the air, by armed aeroplanes against each other. *This fight for the supremacy of the air in future wars will be of the first and greatest importance,* and when it has been won the land and sea forces of the loser will be at such a disadvantage that the war will certainly have to terminate at a much smaller loss in men and money to both sides." It can be said that the predictions in the statement quoted were fully realized during the late war, and the time has now come for them to be lifted to the higher plane of strategic thought. Writing on this, Sir Walter Raleigh says: " With the conquest of the air the task of self-defence for Great Britain has been doubled. It is not to be wondered at that those who were responsible for keeping open the gates of the sea should turn their eyes away from the new duty. But the new duty—command of the air, so to call it—was plainly visible to those who once looked at it. We must keep the highways open, or our freedom is gone. We must command the air. ' I do not say that we wish to do so,' said Capt. Surter, ' but I think we shall be forced to do so.' The whole of our naval history is summed up in that sentence; and the whole of our air policy is foretold."*

The expression "command of the air" is analogous to "command of the sea," and it is as well perhaps to remember that no such condition as absolute command in either of these elements is ever likely to fall to the good fortune of even the most victorious forces.

Air superiority may be defined as " A state of moral and material superiority over the enemy, which prevents him from seriously interfering with hostile air operations, and at the same time denies him the successful employment of his own air forces."

The best that can be done on the sea is to control the sea communications for whatever purpose we require them. The same applies to the air. Air superiority may be said to exist when the nation possessing it can freely and with security use the air routes which are necessary to carry out its operations of war, and at the same time can deny to the enemy the use of such air routes as he may require for his own operations.

It is to be noted that even an established air superiority will never in practice be absolute. No degree of air superiority can secure every point within the radius of action of enemy aircraft against sporadic attack from individual aeroplanes or even flights or squadrons of aeroplanes. Therefore, by air superiority, we do not

War in the Air. Raleigh.

mean that the enemy can do nothing, but that he cannot interfere with our operations in the air, on sea or on land, so seriously as to affect the issue of these operations, and that he cannot carry on his own operations except at such a risk as to make them devoid of any hope of success. In other words, it means that the enemy can no longer attack us effectively, and that he cannot defend all his vital points from the attack of our aircraft.

Air superiority, then, is an essential preliminary to all air operations to be undertaken on a large scale, and a necessary preliminary for ensuring the success of land or sea operations in which air forces are extensively engaged. This brings us to a situation analogous to that of sea warfare when superiority is in dispute. The general conditions may be that the power of neither side preponderates appreciably. Preponderance, of course, will not depend entirely on actual relative strength, either material or moral, but will be influenced by the inter-relation of geographical positions and movable or fixed air bases, and by the strategical value of their situation in regard to the more important objectives in the war area.

Directly or indirectly, the object of air warfare must, in the first instance, always be the securing of air superiority and the subsequent maintenance of that superiority. My purpose is to show that this will only be achieved, and can only be achieved, by fighting.

Superiority in the air will result from a successful and sustained offensive which will bring an enemy's aircraft to action whenever possible by intensive bombing attacks on his aerodromes and other vitally important military objectives, which, apart from the material damage inflicted, have the additional effect of weakening his moral. Here again it may be noted that sporadic efforts will achieve but temporary results. Therefore our action must be in the nature of a sustained effort from which alone we may hope to gain some effects that will last a fair period of time.

Further, in an endeavour to secure superiority we may employ indirect methods, such as attacking an enemy's means of production. The adoption of this course must depend primarily on the degree to which we can hope by such means to affect the issue of the war. Circumstances can only decide our policy, and our course of action in this direction must be determined entirely by the military situation, by the vulnerability of the targets and by their relative value to the enemy.

Apart from the direct pressure to which allusion has been made, the following advantages will result from superiority in the air :—In the first place a commander will obtain "a great liberty of action," since, for while holding the power of covering the movements of his own sea and land forces, he will be well informed as to those of the enemy. An air attack on ports and shipping may be effective in hindering the movement of shipping and aircraft and the importation of food, munitions and merchandise. Further, the enemy's naval squadrons may be provoked, by continuous air attack, to leave the shelter of ports and harbours, and be forced into areas where they must either accept battle or take up a position of strategical disadvantage. On land, enemy troops may be so much harassed and their repose so frequently disturbed that they may be unable to march or fight with the best energy. Traffic, both during the period of concentration for battle and afterwards in the areas behind the fighting forces, may also be interrupted, and the transport of men, supplies and munitions necessary for the fighting efficiency may be rendered so precarious that the position of his troops in battle will be endangered. The menace of attack from the air will, in addition, oblige the enemy to lock up an undue proportion of men, aircraft and artillery in passive defence, and the forces available for active operations will be proportionately reduced. The manifold advantages outlined may appear too difficult of attainment, but there is no doubt, from the experience gained during the late war, that they are all within the power of the nation possessing air superiority.

The following extracts from despatches on the operations during the late war will serve to illustrate the importance of air superiority and some of the benefits which accrue to the power possessing it.

Operations in Palestine. Despatch dated 31/10/18, from Commander-in-Chief, Expeditionary Force:—

"The process of wearing down the enemy's strength in the air has been continuous throughout the summer. Our ascendancy in the air became so marked towards the end of August that only a few of the enemy's aeroplanes were able to fly, with the result that my troops were immune from air attacks during the operations, and the whole strength of the air forces could be concentrated on the enemy in his retreat."

Despatch from the Commander-in-Chief, British armies in France, dated 20/7/18:—

"Throughout the period of active operations our airmen have established and maintained a superiority over the enemy's air forces without parallel since the days of the first Somme battle. Not content with destroying the enemy in the air, they have vigorously attacked his infantry, guns, and transport with bombs and machine-gun fire, and in the fighting south of the Somme in particular gave invaluable assistance to the infantry by these means on numerous occasions."

"The measure of support afforded to the armies in what was a critical period of the war—the last German onslaught in France—cannot be measured in terms of casualties and destruction inflicted upon the attacked. What, perhaps, is of far greater importance is the fact that air superiority over the enemy air forces has an incalculable moral effect on all arms of the Army. Facts justify the statement that to the enemy it neutralized to a very great extent their successes, and to our own troops brought relief and moral support of immeasurable wealth."

Superiority may not be gained in all areas. It may so happen that superiority may be gained in one area and lost in another. It will be for the strategist to decide which areas are the most vital to the success of the general operations, and to ensure that the air forces within those areas are of sufficient strength or quality to gain and retain the superiority.

The important fact which differentiates the air arm from naval or military forces is its ability to operate over wide areas, and if any part is defeated it can be rapidly replaced—provided that the facilities exist for training and production and that these are in no way interfered with. This fact alone makes it difficult to ensure maintaining superiority. We can assume, therefore, as a safe axiom that air superiority will not be gained without heavy fighting, and a considerable period will have to elapse before that superiority is gained by either belligerent. That it may be of temporary duration is also manifest.

Speaking generally, it may be said that future wars will commence with great air activity " in advance of contact, either upon land or sea, and victory will incline to that power which is able first to achieve, and later to maintain, his superiority in the air." Although this may be taken as a general rule applicable in cases where the frontiers of the belligerents are contiguous or where the possession of air bases renders it possible for aircraft to reach objectives in enemy territory across the narrow seas, yet in other cases, where the distances separating the belligerents are so great that aircraft are unable to operate except from carriers, this can hardly be so. In such a war between either America or Japan, or Great Britain and either of these, war at sea would predominate from the commencement of hostilities and before the main air forces of either side could come into action. This much, however, can be said with certainty, that the side that is able to utilize the major portion of his air forces in support of such operations will possess considerable advantage over the other.

Air Combat.

The supreme importance of superiority in tactical skill in air fighting cannot be over-estimated. The fact that aircraft possess three-dimensional movement will necessitate the evolution of tactical formations in air fighting. The development of armament and the capabilities of future types of aircraft can alone decide the tactical formations which are best. It is not, therefore, possible to lay down any fundamental principles, as it is considered that this subject will be dependent upon the course of future developments.

Moral.

We must at all times aim at a moral ascendancy over our enemy. As was demonstrated during the Great War, in which aircraft were employed for the first time, the war in the air was an uninterrupted race for moral ascendancy. It was almost a daily occurrence for one or a few machines to attack whole squadrons, or a squadron of bombers to be attacked and to keep up a running fight against overwhelming numbers of fighters. It was to such actions that we can attribute the constant moral ascendancy over the enemy. Whole squadrons would sometimes be destroyed in this manner. The using up of units piecemeal, which is always an evil, became on occasions a necessary evil. Commanders suffered that evil while reducing it to its least possible limits. In the constant race for superiority of moral it was necessary to attack, however weak one's forces. Indeed, one may say that the principle "the weaker one is the more one should attack" applies most strongly to air warfare. Their continuous aim at moral ascendancy, to be maintained at all costs, kept the enemy on the defensive in spite of his possessing at times superior numbers and better equipment.

"The inexorable fact is that, when opposed by a capable adversary, the unprepared nation is invariably compelled by force of circumstances to put its troops into battle piecemeal and *before they have been properly* *trained to fight, with the result that losses are incurred out of all proportion to the progress made in winning the war*, while the lives thus sacrificed are usually amongst the best which the nation possesses."*

I think it is true to say that during the Great War we were often driven by force of circumstances to put air forces into battle before the personnel had been properly trained. Our unpreparedness in this respect was unavoidable, for this new arm was then in its initial stages of development. The subsequent progress made in air fighting and tactics necessitated a higher standard of training. This is borne out in a statement which appears in a White Paper presented to Parliament in April, 1919. In the early days of the war the urgency of the demand rendered it necessary for pilots to go overseas immediately they had reached the minimum standard of efficiency, and *five* hours solo flying qualified a pilot for France. This minimum time was gradually raised in 1917 to *thirty-five* hours, and in 1918 very few pilots had done less than *fifty* hours before they were sent on active service. Apart from the actual instruction in flying, pilots and observers received specialized training for the particular work they had to do in connection with air fighting, reconnaissance, bombing, and the many duties of naval and army work. Without the improved efficiency obtained from this longer period of training, the attainment of air superiority would not have been possible. As further developments take place in air fighting and in all air work, a still higher standard will be required. The necessity of preparedness to meet these conditions will therefore greatly increase. We must avoid being compelled by force of circumstances that can be foreseen, to put air forces into active operations before the personnel have been properly trained.

The attainment of air superiority lies firstly, then, in the skill and moral of the personnel, and secondly in the superior performance of the machines and the

*From Private to Field-Marshal. Field-Marshal Sir Wm. Robertson.

efficiency of their armament. Superior machines and armament are, however, of little value if the personnel using them be not of the highest order. In the long run, it is the man who decides the issue. No superiority in material can compensate for inferiority of training, skill or moral. Similarly, superiority in numbers of aircraft will not alone determine the degree of air superiority that can be obtained over an adversary. Throughout history it has been incontestable that not by superiority of numbers, or weapons, but by the superior moral and fighting qualities of our soldiers and seamen that our greatest victories have been won. And so it will be with the future battles of the air. Even the most cursory study of the war of 1914-18 proves this claim. By the very nature of its work, the air service demands the highest standard of moral in the individual. "Moral," and all that this vitally important word implies, is mainly a psychological factor. Its standard is built up during the course and processes of daily life. The habits of life persist in moments of the utmost stress. Moral force is, therefore, one of the supreme factors of warfare; without it the material, however good, is next to useless. Battle is really a contest between two opposing wills. Victory does not so much depend upon deadly weapons as upon that invisible weapon, the will to conquer. None can reach a true conception of military affairs who disregards the moral factor, without which mere superiority of numbers or of strength is comparatively of little value.

Matériel is and always will be subordinate to personnel. The last thing we want to do is to subordinate life to mechanism. As Sir Walter Raleigh points out, "improvements in mechanical science, to be of any use in war, depend on the skill and practice of those who use them."

The efficiency of *matériel*, whether in its design, construction, or handling, is entirely dependent on efficient personnel.

In times of peace we are apt to look on the development of *matériel* as the beginning and the end of progress. Wherever the training of personnel has not kept pace with the development of *matériel*, there is a rude awakening in the day when they are tested.

IMPORTANCE OF PRODUCTION AND RESERVES.

Progress in civil aviation will have a very great bearing on Service considerations. Apart from the direct benefits which such progress will bring an empire power in particular, commercial air activity will be of very great importance in its effect on the defence of this country and the Empire as a whole. Civil aviation will not only create a reserve of pilots and ground personnel, but also add to the facilities for more rapid expansion and output of material. It will, in addition, build up air bases which may prove of considerable strategic importance, and greatly increase the mobility of the air forces.

Expansion for war is an important question which requires further consideration. In the first few months after the outbreak of war, the existing aircraft industry will be the only source of supply. This period will be succeeded by an even longer one, during which these firms will expand and turn out machines at a steadily-increasing rate. If the war be prolonged, the aircraft industry proper will be augmented by the inclusion of additional works adapted from their normal peace work to that of aircraft production—such as the motor industry and kindred factories. When this latter stage is reached, the rate of production of aircraft in a highly industrialized country like the United Kingdom will be very great.

Production of aircraft during the late war cannot be taken as a basis upon which we can form even an approximate estimate of present or future production. This must necessarily depend, amongst other things, on the progress of aviation, the scientific changes in aircraft, and many other factors of no less importance.

Whatever may be the conditions that render greater production possible, it is questionable whether the rate of expansion of fighting units that was witnessed during the last war will be exceeded or even approached. We have to compare the conditions which prevail at the present day with those of ten years ago. Although losses due to non-enemy action may show a marked decrease, it cannot be said that this is likely to offset the increased losses due to the intensity of air fighting and to the greater range and destructive power of air armaments which will inevitably take place. One must not forget, also, that any increase in the effectiveness of anti-aircraft ground defences will add to the losses.

An ex-Air Minister has stated that "the casualties in the air in the next war had been calculated at 80 per cent. per month, and any war between two great countries would be a war in the air and would be won by the country which could most readily replace casualties."

When one comes to consider, therefore, the question of expansion in war, these unknown factors will play a great part in determining the rate of increase in fighting strength that will be possible. One must not forget, also, that any increase in losses to material due to fighting will increase the losses in the crews, and the problem of the replacement of trained personnel will probably be more acute in the next than in the late war. Supply on the material side may easily outstrip that of trained personnel. Those who imagine, therefore, that the next war will see more and more aircraft employed are likely to be disillusioned. Changes are both rapid and revolutionary and we cannot with any certainty predict the extent to which these changes will alter the whole conduct of air warfare.

The losses in the first few weeks of air fighting are bound to be heavy, and the power which can make good those losses at the outset will gain the advantage. Peace organization and preparations for war must allow for the replacement of these losses both in personnel and *matériel* and the immediate expansion of the force on mobilization. The success of a campaign will depend largely upon this basic organization.

From these arguments it is seen how important it will be to have the necessary trained reserves of personnel available besides the *matériel*. The country that possesses the greater facilities for aircraft production will have a distinct advantage over another whose production is smaller. It will be of little avail to the former if that organization for production is not immediately available and if the plans are not such as to ensure the use of the whole of the manufacturing resources to the best advantage.

"There can be no continuity of evolution without demand, for demand is the incentive of supply and the most efficient supply is obtained through competition. To create a general demand for civil air traffic is to lay the foundations of air strategy and, without these foundations, no great military progress can be expected. Once aircraft are a commercial asset, then strategy is assured, for not only will competition improve the equipment, but also the organization and the personnel, without which it will not be possible to effect a rapid expansion of military flying from its peace basis on the outbreak of war. . . . It must not be forgotten that this expansion equally depends for its success on the then existing Air Force being of a sufficient strength and efficiency to take advantage of the civil organization."*
Air power, like sea power, to be effective and permanent must be based on a sound and economic development for peace uses.

We can, I think, safely assume that where two countries are at war and where both are able to carry out bombing attacks, the issue will rest more on the question of "reserves" than on any other factor. Losses will be heavy on both sides, and success (the gaining of air superiority and the maintenance of such superiority) will, to a large degree, be dependent upon

* *The Fiends of the Air.* Anon.

the "reserves" available for employment during the first few months of hostilities.

It is essential that reserves of aircraft, engines and spares are sufficient to meet losses for the period that must inevitably elapse between the outbreak of war and the time when production can reach the stage of replenishing losses. The length of this period will depend mainly on the organization that is set up in peace time. Such organization must ensure that on the outbreak of war all available resources in aircraft production are immediately turned to good account and that our requirements can be fully met with the minimum loss of time. Arrangements for the expansion of the aircraft industry must also be precise. These plans must be subject to annual scrutiny, in order that they may fulfil present or future needs and conform with the latest developments. The Commander-in-Chief in France emphasized this point when, in a despatch dated December 23rd, 1916, he wrote : " 'The maintenance of mastery (superiority) in the air, which is essential, entails a constant and liberal supply of the most up-to-date machines, without which even the most skilful pilots cannot succeed."

Again, in a later despatch, dated December 25th, 1917, from the same source, this point is still further emphasized : "The enemy shows no signs of relaxing his endeavours in this department of war. Whilst acknowledging therefore most fully the great effort that has been made to meet the ever-increasing demands of this most important Service, I feel it my duty once more to point out that the position that has been won by the skill, courage and devotion of our pilots can only be maintained by a liberal supply of the most efficient machines."

In conclusion, the following quotation from the report of the American Aviation Commission presented to Congress in 1920, forms a just appreciation of the experiences gained during the war. The report states :

" That no sudden creation of air equipment to meet a national emergency already at hand is possible. It has been proved within the experience of every nation engaged in the war (1914-18) that two years or more of high pressure effort have been needed to achieve the quantity production of aircraft, aircraft engines, and accessory equipment. The training of personnel, including engineering, production, inspection, maintenance and operating forces—covering some fifty distinct trades and some seventy-five industries—has proved itself a stupendous task when undertaken upon the basis of war emergency alone."

Air Chief Marshal Trenchard, commenting on the above conclusion, says : "It must always be remembered that mobilization does not end war, but only begins it, and that therefore additional provision must be made against war wastage. The difficulties of the Air Service are abnormal in this respect. The nature of its work makes wastage high, both in personnel and *matériel*. The necessity for immediate and intensive training on a greatly increased scale adds to this. Great reserves of *matériel* present a peculiarly difficult problem, since, in addition to being very costly to provide and store, a great deal of such *matériel* deteriorates rapidly, whilst all is liable to become obsolete owing to the rapid development of aeronautical science."

The question of reserves is one which presents very great difficulties, and, it is hardly necessary to point out, that it is one which is of the utmost importance when war breaks out, for, unless reserves of aircraft and engines are immediately available to replace losses, a country will find itself in a precarious position. In point of fact, it becomes obvious that its position in the air after the first few weeks of heavy air fighting will be irretrievably lost. It is more than likely that the first few weeks will decide the issue as far as the air is concerned, and reserves, both *matériel* and personnel, might conceivably be the decisive factor. The difficulties presented are not, however, insuperable, and in course of time may disappear completely, for these difficulties may be said to be transitory.

In the meantime, development will proceed. It may be with less rapidity than was the case during the late war. Design of aircraft and engines, although more stabilized, will always be subject to the process of evolution. We are always inclined to imagine that the stage has been reached beyond which no progress is possible. This is far from being true, and in war the progress and change are more rapid and revolutionary in so far as weapons and modes of fighting are concerned. Principles of war, however, are unaffected by such changes. It would seem, therefore, that, although development of aircraft will in the not far distant future be stabilized to a degree, yet there is the probability—the greater on account of their infancy—that aircraft have yet to undergo some revolutionary stages before anything approaching stabilization is reached. The period of ten to fifteen years is perhaps an optimistic estimate of the time this process will take.

There appears at the moment no likelihood of stability in design being reached for some considerable time. Until such time as stability is more or less established, large reserves appear to be out of the question, for the *matériel* will soon be out of date and will need frequent replacement. In pursuing such a policy, expense appears prohibitive, and more particularly because there is no market for these out-of-date machines. Nevertheless, it appears possible to have a reasonably strong reserve available, for each year normal wastage demands replacement and is probably sufficient to keep a certain number of aircraft manufacturing firms in a state of regular production and experiment, particularly if subsidized by the Government.

Growth of civil aviation will cause still further production and increased plant, which, in the event of war, must be at the disposal of the nation to replace losses and as a basis for expansion. The size and potential output of a country's aircraft industry will be the prime factor on the outbreak of war, and it is during the first two or three months of hostilities that the demand is likely to outstrip the production. It behoves us, therefore, to be prepared, and to make plans covering this most vital period.

Mobilization must proceed with the utmost smoothness and rapidity. Every hour saved in this process will be of vital importance. Movements will be so rapid that no country can afford to allow several days for the mobilization of even the whole of its air resources on the outbreak of war. A considerable proportion of the air forces, varying according to circumstances, must be kept by all Powers in a state of readiness to go into action at a moment's notice. Organized force is the determining feature. The Air Force is itself the strategic position.

CHAPTER III.

(1) OFFENCE AND DEFENCE.

"A vigorous offensive, strategical as well as tactical, is always the safest method of conducting operations."

ONE of the notorious principles of war, familiar to all who have read books about war, is that a merely defensive attitude is a losing attitude. The man who is thoroughly versed in the doctrine of the initiative—which he knows by instinct and experience, not by the reading of learned treatises—has the most important of all attributes at his command in which to deal successfully with his opponents. "The experience of the war," says Sir Walter Raleigh,* "from beginning to end, taught the old lesson of the supreme value of the offensive. The lesson was quickly learned and put to proof by our air forces on all fronts" (of which examples will be given hereafter). "The air forces, from the first, sought every opportunity for offensive action. Those who commanded the air forces divined the right doctrine, and practised it, and established it in use, *thereby securing for the Air Force the liberty to use its power to the best advantage.*"

It is perhaps difficult to determine the point at which defence, as applied to the air, really begins. It is important to realize that all air action is offensive in character and there is no such thing perhaps as taking up a defensive position. What it really comes down to, then, is this. Is it our object to defend or is it to attack? If our course of action is determined purely by what the enemy does and is undertaken with a view to preventing him from attaining *his* object, then our action is a defensive one.

War in the Air. Raleigh.

In this category falls the air defence of particular localities. The adoption of a defensive policy—essential for those points that are vital and are open to serious air attack—should never be voluntarily accepted, but is necessitated by force of circumstances. It will rarely happen that one side has greater advantages than another in this respect. A waiting policy will not only give the enemy the initiative, but also react on the moral both of the force itself and that of all other arms. Such a policy may serve to satisfy public opinion, but that alone is not sufficient justification for departing from the principle of offensive action unless such action is of vital importance and does in reality achieve its object—the defeat of those forces against which the defence has been organized. To satisfy these political and military necessities in one and the same system is a difficult task. We cannot wholly neglect the former, but their interests can best be secured by concentrating on the military side. Field-Marshal Sir William Robertson emphasizes the fact " that when war is afoot the requirements of home defence, whether on land, on sea, or in the air, will, except perhaps in the case of a great crisis, such as that which occurred in March, 1918, invariably have to be given precedence over requirements connected with operations abroad.

He further emphasizes the fact that " the best defence against air attacks at home is, as everybody knows, to keep the hostile airmen employed abroad, either in defending their own country or on the fronts where the opposing main armies are engaged. But while, in theory, it may be correct to give chief consideration to the maintenance of superior air forces on the fighting fronts, in practice suitable defence against air attacks at home must first be provided, and sufficient resources to satisfy both purposes will seldom be forthcoming. They were not in 1916-17, and the General Staff, in deciding what should be done, were sometimes not allowed by the Government to give to the needs of the field armies that priority of treatment which, in their opinion, they should have been accorded. More than once in 1917, when air raids were made on London, air squadrons were kept back in England which might preferably have been sent to France, and sometimes squadrons in France already were ordered to return."*

Air attack to be successful must be in the form of a sustained effort. Half-hearted measures will achieve nothing. Defence must be supported with the utmost energy. In all these operations we must constantly keep in mind the ultimate military objective of war—the destruction of the enemy's forces. No one will admit that a purely air defensive can accomplish the defeat of an enemy air force. On the contrary, it might sooner or later allow the enemy time in which to succeed in attaining his object, even though he were the weaker. Hence the conclusion that the offensive form alone, whether it be resorted to at once or only after the defensive, can lead to results, and must therefore always be adopted, at least in the end. It might almost be laid down as an air maxim that there can be no successful air defence unless it be supported by offensive operations.

We must endeavour to fix in our minds the probable trend of air operations in war under varying circumstances and the effect of such circumstances upon their character.

In air warfare it will be impossible either to establish a defence or to develop offence fully without securing "superiority in the air." This superiority can only be attained by aggressive action against the enemy's air forces, and against those objectives of strategical or tactical importance for the defence of which the enemy will be obliged to utilize part of his air units.

Furthermore, we shall always find, as we found during the late war, that however stoically we aim at defence the most effective means of gaining security is by offensive operations.

It may therefore so happen that offensive operations will be undertaken by both sides simultaneously, and

* *Soldiers and Statesmen*, Vol. II.

the side which is able to maintain the more vigorous and sustained offensive will eventually force his adversary to the defensive.

A very important fact and one to be constantly borne in mind is that the air possesses no defensive frontiers, and that aircraft, within their radius of action, are at liberty to operate where and when they like.

There are no physical features which prevent aircraft from being moved in any direction. We cannot, as it were, "choose our ground" or take up a defensive position so strong that it cannot be turned or one that must be broken down before the enemy can reach his objective. The advantage of surprise is therefore with the attack, and the doctrine that "where the defence is sound and well-designed the advantage of surprise is against the attack" does not apply to air defence. This is intensified in the case of the separation of the belligerents by sea, and where the frontiers to be defended are extensive, which facts facilitate surprise attack. It is not intended to imply that the whole of our forces should be employed in offensive action away from the area open to attack by enemy forces, but that those of our forces utilized for defensive operations must be supported sooner or later by offensive action.

Circumstances alone will dictate what strength we should employ on either of these operations, but the success of the defence will depend on the extent to which, by offensive action, we are able to support it. The characteristic of the offence is that it makes the attack instead of accepting it. This was evidenced in 1914-1918 by the fact that our air victories were almost if not always won by attacking the enemy in the vicinity of his own bases.

A commander who can take the initiative has the ability to concentrate at the spot desired, whereas passive defence more often means the dispersion of his forces in an endeavour to cover too many danger points at once. These principles of strategy apply more strongly perhaps to the employment of air than to either naval or military forces.

The "initiative" in the employment of such "mobile" forces is therefore of very great strategical and tactical importance. On the other hand, the mobility possessed by aircraft does to some extent allow a flexibility of defence, although this cannot be said to outweigh the disadvantages or the difficulties to be encountered.

Offensive action by aircraft comes under two headings, combat and attack. The first relates to fighting in the air, and the second to the attack in the other elements. These types of offensive action are related. The former is directly undertaken with the object of gaining "superiority in the air," whilst the latter *depends* on "superiority in the air" for its success.

The first war in the air bore out the effectiveness of the principle of the offensive as it was applied by the Allied air forces, and it was due chiefly to its rigorous application that we were enabled to secure that superiority over the enemy in the face, at times, of adverse circumstances and inferiority in numbers. Whatever the aim, therefore, this principle must be pursued with the greatest energy, and success exploited to the utmost. Only thus can the enemy be forced into the disadvantageous policy of conforming to our operations and abandoning his own plans. No opportunity must be afforded him of taking the initiative and imposing his will on us, nor must time be given him to recover from our blows or to prepare to meet them.

Vice-Admiral Sir Reginald Bacon, in his despatch on the "Operations of the Dover Patrol," says:—

" It is equally advantageous to maintain the offensive in the air as it is to do so on land or at sea. It is with considerable satisfaction, therefore, that I am able to report that, with only one exception, all the aeroplanes destroyed were fought over the enemy's territory and that all the aeroplanes were brought down into waters off the enemy's coast."

Early in the war it became apparent that no form of sedentary defence could ever succeed, but that fighting in the air was the ultimate rôle of the opposing air forces and that this was the only means of gaining decisive results.

"The strategy of the sea," writes Admiral Bacon, "—to seek out and fight the enemy's fleet—held good in the air. It became clear that, unless the air forces of the country were sufficient to do this, and do it with ultimate success, all arms of both the naval and military forces would be hopelessly handicapped as compared with those of the enemy."*

The same author states that the ever-growing value of aircraft was being emphasized daily in the official *communiqués* both of the Allies and the enemy, and that it was no exaggeration to state that the success of the Allies on the Somme was largely due to the success of the Allied machines in forcing the enemy aircraft to act entirely on the defensive during the three months prior to the attack. From the commencement of the Battle of the Somme on July 1st, 1916, our air forces maintained a consistent and continuous offensive air policy over the enemy's lines. This offensive policy, which was maintained right up to the signing of the Armistice, proved most valuable and undoubtedly gave the British superiority in the air.

Admiral Sir Reginald Bacon adds that it was recognized by the leading military authorities (to which the *communiqués* bear witness) that, in the event of the enemy having air superiority, successful military operations would be much more expensive in manpower.

The efficacy of an offensive as opposed to a defensive policy is summed up in the following extract from an official report on air warfare on the Western Front, 1914 to 1918: "The idea of a defensive policy was never subscribed to by the Higher Command of the Royal Flying Corps. The latter had always fostered a vigorous offensive spirit and the Battle of Verdun was to prove that the best defensive policy was an incessant

The Dover Patrol, Vol. II. Admiral Sir Reginald Bacon.

offensive. When the operations at Verdun began, the French front in that sector was sparsely served with aeroplanes. A concentration was at once made and a continuous offensive in the air was made with all available forces. Fighting formations flew well behind the enemy's lines and attacked his machines whenever they were seen. This policy was so successful that after a time the enemy seemed to give up the struggle, and the French fighting squadrons were split up to provide escorts for the Corps squadrons. The result was that the German Air Service, having learned its lesson from the French, adopted a strong offensive, and for a time the French were unable to prevent formidable hostile raids. The French fighting squadrons were again grouped under a single commander, and resumed their offensive beyond the whole front. Once more this method resulted in superiority for the French, and this was so complete that Corps machines were able to resume their work unprotected."

The principles of war, " Concentration " and " Offensive," are thus fully demonstrated in the foregoing narrative. Our own concentration and intense and unremitting offensive carried out prior to and during the Somme Battle later in the same year further vindicated the policy pursued. The superiority established over the enemy was complete.

Summing up the results of these operations of the Somme Battle, the report concludes : " The moral effect which was achieved did not lay only over the enemy's air forces, for by this time superiority had been well established, but particularly over his troops on the ground, an effect that was to outlive the war itself."

The object of all war is victory, and a purely defensive attitude can never bring about a successful decision. The idea that a war can be won by standing on the defensive and waiting for the enemy to attack is a dangerous fallacy, which owes its inception to the desire to evade the price of victory. It is an axiom that decisive success in battle can be gained only by a vigorous offensive. The principle here stated has long been recognized as being fundamental and is based on the universal teaching of military history in all ages. The course of air operations of the late and first war in which aircraft have been engaged has proved that teaching to be of even greater import to this new arm. Let us consider in the light of this war the facts upon which this axiom is based.

Apart from the special difficulties added to the problems of air defence as compared with defence on sea or land, and those common to all forms of defence, a defensive rôle sooner or later brings about a distinct lowering of the moral of the air personnel (and, incidentally, to the personnel of Navy and Army alike), who imagine that the enemy must be the better man, or at least more numerous, better equipped with "aircraft and *matériel*" or other mechanical aids to victory. Once the mass of pilots becomes possessed of such ideas, superiority in the air is as good as lost.

An air force to gain its object must, whenever geographical or other considerations permit, maintain a constant air offensive over the enemy's territory. Only by such action can the enemy's resistance be broken down. Air defence that is essential must be provided for the most vital points or areas, and must be subordinate to the necessity of keeping the nation's striking power intact in support of the more important military operations.

" The steps taken for national defence should be such as will render both home and foreign possessions, as well as commerce, industries and other national interests reasonably secure against aggression.

" The means of national defence may be defined as the provision of armed forces uniformly organized and not only available for timely employment to secure national territories and interests, but also adequate for this purpose.

" A nation, further, will endeavour to carry war into the heart of the country of the most important of its enemies, with the object of protecting its own territory by attacking those of the enemy."*

If we examine this statement in the light of defence against air attack, we shall observe a fundamental axiom upon which the measures of air defence will be framed. This principle figures largely in our existing organization adapted to meet the menace of air attack on this country. Our main protection must come from our striking force. The safety of a country will be best secured by striking hard at the enemy, who will then be so concerned to protect his own interests as to be unable to spare forces from its defence.

Although we can agree that the best defence lies in attacking the enemy in the manner indicated, it is important to remember that defence for vital points must be provided if they are open to attack.

What, for instance, might have been the result if we had made no effective provision for the defence of this country against the airship and aeroplane raids? It would have emboldened the enemy to undertake many more raids and employ far greater strength, and, as mentioned elsewhere, these would have come at a time when we were feeling the severe economic pressure of the German submarine campaign.

Apart, therefore, from the direct obligation imposed upon us, this defence indirectly enabled us to defeat those enemy air forces employed in attacks on this country and to achieve a further superiority in the air. Whether we could ultimately have defeated these raids by an earlier energetic offensive against Germany is a matter of conjecture, but the results obtained by our later action would seem to justify the conclusion that it might. Other considerations, however, enter into the argument, and what " might have been " in war is a dangerous basis upon which to attempt to draw safe conclusions.

Any air forces employed in the defence must necessarily have as their object the defeat of the enemy's air

*The Direction of War. W. D. Bird.

forces which threaten the area or point attacked. We must realize that, no matter how clear our positive aim, we cannot develop an aggressive line of strategy to the full without some dissipation of force of a defensive nature. Our strategy must therefore be both offensive and defensive. Whatever may be our decision, the ultimate end must always be kept in view—the destruction of the enemy's air forces and the furtherance of our naval and military operations, the combined strategy of the three armed forces having as its object the defeat of the enemy nation.

By July, 1917, although raids on England still continued, it became apparent that the policy of offence abroad rather than of passive defence at home was correct. Our continued bombing of enemy aerodromes and our air offensive in France were producing good results. The great damage done to aerodromes caused serious disorganization. It was also evident that the enemy was being forced to divert a considerable portion of his bombing machines against the aerodromes from which these attacks originated. The net result was that a great part of the enemy's bombing power which might have been used against England was diverted against our aerodromes abroad. Results similar to these were attained by our attacks on Germany in 1918.

Air defence of Great Britain or any other country is not confined solely to the defence of industrial areas. This may be of considerable importance, but the whole problem must be treated from a much wider aspect if the defence measures are to be sound. The peculiar circumstances of each country must be considered. It may not be the industrial areas of Great Britain, but London, the docks, the ports, our shipping and our naval bases that are the vital points that must be protected.

(2) PRINCIPLE OF CONCENTRATION.

It is easy for us to see in the light of after events the mistakes that actually were made in past wars, but we cannot appraise the mistakes that might or would have been made if a different course of action had been adopted.

The dictates of strategy often lose sight of one great fundamental reason that is generally responsible for the chief mistakes and difficulties in our strategy. It lies in the fact that, being a great Empire, our responsibilities in war are world-wide. Earl Grey* has recorded it as his opinion that the chief mistakes in strategy may be summarized in two words: " Side-shows." Having world-wide responsibilities does, however, make it impossible for all of them to be avoided. But Earl Grey remarks further that it is a true criticism that we did not in the late war sufficiently *concentrate* attention on the one cardinal point: that it was the German Army which had to be beaten and that this could be done only on the Western Front. For us to attempt it anywhere else, he says, was to give the Germans the advantage of interior and safer lines of communication compared with our own. Had this been grasped continuously as the central fact of the war, the side-shows—Gallipoli, Bagdad, Salonika—would either never have been undertaken or would have been kept *within smaller dimensions*.

One may not entirely agree with this latter point, for there can be little doubt that the Gallipoli enterprise was well conceived, but lacked both surprise and the necessary concentration of effort. Had we kept our other side-shows in the East within smaller dimensions and concentrated on this more important enterprise, it might have succeeded. If it had succeeded it is only reasonable to suppose that it would have ended our commitments in Mesopotamia and Palestine and left us free to concentrate the whole of our efforts on the Western Front.

Field-Marshal Sir William Robertson sums up the situation in a few words when he says that " it is no exaggeration to say that every mistake we had made in

Twenty-five Years. Earl Grey of Fallodon.

our wars with France more than a hundred years before had been repeated. We had committed ourselves to expeditions on a vast scale and in remote theatres, which were strategically unsound, had never been properly thought out, and in the Dardanelles alone had cost us considerably over 100,000 casualties. The false direction thus given to our strategy imperilled the chances of ultimate success.

"It is," he continues, "one of the first principles of war that all available resources should be concentrated at the 'decisive' point—*that is, at the place where the main decision of the war is to be fought out.* There may be a difference of opinion as to where that point should be, but there should never be more than one such point at a time, and once the selection is made, no departure from the principle just mentioned is admissible except (a) when it becomes necessary to detach forces for the protection of interests vital to oneself; or (b) when by detaching them the enemy will be compelled as a counter-measure to send a still larger detachment in order to protect interests which are vital to him."

It is as well not to ignore the other side of the picture, but to remember that the possession of an Empire with world-wide interests to protect, makes the question of side-shows an important factor in our strategic problems and necessitates our undertaking campaigns in violation of the principle of concentration. However much we may try to avoid them, the fact remains they cannot all be entirely ignored. In this connection, there is a great deal of truth in the following passage taken from Sir Walter Raleigh's book, "War in the Air." Although perhaps the particular operation to which he refers cannot, strictly speaking, be taken as a side-show, but rather an operation undertaken with a view not so much to carrying out a diversion, but in support of the major operations conducted in the main theatre of war, his remarks nevertheless apply to those side-shows in other theatres of war, around which there has been so much controversy and criticism. He writes: "Such critics condemn all such adventures as side-shows. They may be right; but it is always to be remembered that the national character is seen at its best in solitary adventures of this kind, and that the British Empire, from the first, was built up on side-shows—many of them unauthorized by the Government.* The experience of the war, and of former wars, proves only that these enterprises *lose a great part of their value if they are timidly designed or half-heartedly executed.* To condemn them out and out is to prefer the German plan of empire, which depends wholly on central initiative and central control, to the sporadic energy of the British Empire, which can never be killed by a blow aimed at the centre, *for its life is in every part.* Military theory, based as it is chiefly on the great campaigns of continental conquerors, has so impressed some of its British students that they forget their own nature, renounce their pride, and cheapen their dearest possessions."

In the employment of air forces, I can see no reason which will detract from the principles outlined in the above. In point of fact, it appears to me that such concentration is of even greater import in our handling of air forces, if for no other reason than that they are unable to take up a defensive position so strong as to make it reasonably secure against enemy penetration. Numbers will therefore play an important rôle in the attainment of our object. With air forces, one thing I think is certain, and that is, there will be an increased desire for "side-shows." We must guard against the temptation at all costs.

Concentration in military text-books is defined as " Concentration of superior force, moral and material, at the decisive time and place, and its ruthless employment in the battle, are essential for the achievement of success."

*It would be as well to remember that members of the Government have since been the chief supporters and originators of such operations.

Some confusion is bound to arise from an analysis of this term. In order, therefore, to clear our minds, it can, I think, be taken that the definition of this principle is, strictly speaking, meant to be applied to strategical distribution.

How can we effect such concentration in so far as air forces are concerned? In what state can air forces be said to be concentrated as intended by this principle? In order to arrive at a decision on this point, it is necessary to discuss more fully the definition given.

Concentration as applied to strategical distribution means " coherent disposal about a strategical centre," and this expression would seem to give us the more exact working definition that we require. Our object may well be to cover the widest possible area either in attack or defence, and provided our forces are based about a common centre they may still be said to be concentrated. The meaning of the term " concentration" in the definition is analogous to that which Mahan has described for naval forces. " Such," says Mahan, " is concentration reasonably understood—not huddled together like a drove of sheep, *but distributed with regard to a common purpose,* and linked together by the effectual energy of a single will." If we take those words in *italics* (the *italics* are mine) as forming the true definition of strategical concentration of air forces, we shall have a very clear and correct conception of what exactly it is that we require to bring about.

The most distant and widely-dispersed points must be kept in view as possible objectives of the enemy. Air forces, on account of their mobility and great range of action, are able to operate from widely-dispersed bases in support of a common purpose. This allows far greater flexibility in the distribution of these forces.

In so far as considerations of bases will admit, the largest possible force should be collected in the area where it can most conveniently be used to inflict the greatest harm on the enemy; where success is most probable and where, if victorious, success will bring the greatest advantages.

It is of the utmost importance to concentrate a sufficient force to ensure the achievement of the object. Spasmodic attacks by small numbers of aircraft can achieve but little. Lack of concentration at the right time may result in defeat or affect seriously the air, sea and land operations.

The following examples will serve to show the importance of this axiom. The first is taken from Admiral Sir Reginald Bacon's book, "The Dover Patrol" (Vol. II), in which he records the effort made by the Germans against our air base at Dunkirk. He writes: "The enemy had many times dropped considerable numbers of heavy bombs on the Depot, with varying success, but actually very little serious damage was occasioned until the end of September, 1917, when a determined and almost successful effort to wipe it out was made. The attacks commenced on the night of September 27th and continued over the nights of September 29th and October 1st, 2nd and 3rd. Over 600 bombs were dropped, nearly all of very heavy calibre. The engine shops and carpenters' shops were completely burnt out, together with many of the smaller workshops and sheds, and the explosion of one of the bomb dumps which was hit at the same time added to the extent of the disaster. This effectively stopped all further work at this base, and necessitated a new base being equipped." This attack, he says, was an apt illustration of what could be done by intensive bombing. The same author later refers to a determined attack by an Allied fleet of 41 machines ("for those days a very imposing total"*) on the German aerodrome at Houtare. This raid resulted in very considerable damage.

I have heard it stated that a separate air force engaged upon operations which it conceives conducive to the winning of a war may be disposed so that it will not furnish the Navy or Army with the air forces they need. But I submit that the very need of the Navy or Army is a strong and united Air Force. The operations of the

*February, 1916.

Navy and Army will be affected by the success or otherwise of the whole of our air forces. To split those forces into distinct branches would involve grave risk of being beaten in detail.

An army embarked for overseas operations depends for the success of its operations on the whole of our Fleet and not on that particular portion of it which may have been set aside for its immediate protection. It depends on the power of the Fleet to prevent the enemy's fleet from interfering with the Army's operations. So with air forces. Both Navy and Army are dependent upon our ability to utilize the whole of our strength in the air in opposing these air forces of the enemy. It may be that the enemy will choose to concentrate the whole of his air forces in support of his operations at sea or on land. If in support of his sea operations, we must concentrate a sufficient air force to ensure the defeat of his air forces. If in support of his land operations, our forces must be equal to the task. Circumstances must therefore dictate the policy to be pursued in the utilization of our air forces to the best advantage. Their employment must depend on the strategic situation. In any case, they must be adequate to ensure the success of our sea or land operations, or for the defence of the country and the Empire against air attack.

Any division of our forces leads to conflicting views as to their ultimate employment. Direction must therefore be in one hand. Two separate commands mean inflexibility and with it dispersion of force. Dispersion will not only minimize the prospect of victory by reducing the numbers and resources available for action in any given area, but will afford to the enemy an opportunity of attacking and defeating our forces in detail.

It must be remembered that in the late war no air force was fully developed. Concentration of effort was therefore hardly possible, even at the end. Strategically it may be said that the forces in France were concentrated with the object of defeating the enemy's air forces and assisting the land operations.

In the future, whether in regard to air fighting or bombing operations, concentration of effort will be essential to air success. Allied preponderance in aircraft to a great extent prevented our suffering defeat in the air and reduced the risks that were run in dispersing our air effort. This dispersion was equally noticeable with the Germans. An analysis of the air successes both on the Allied and German sides, demonstrates that these could be attributed in the first place to a greater concentration of force and effort directed to the attainment of the particular object in view. If the objective of our attack is vital to the enemy, then we must ensure that the force we employ against it is of such strength as to ensure success.

To show what is meant by this, let us take a few illustrations arising from the late war. The records show the futility of many of the bombing attacks undertaken by the Germans on this country and France, and of our own efforts on such targets as the submarine bases on the Belgian coast. What might not the Germans have achieved if they had concentrated their bombing attacks for weeks on end on such important points as our Army's bases of supply or on one important English port during the submarine crisis?

Again, what would have been the result if we had concentrated the major portion of our bombing squadrons for one week in day and night attacks on the submarine bases at Bruges, Zeebrugge and Ostend? Some tangible results would have been attained, whereas, with only a few squadrons employed consistently on this task, we were never able to attain results commensurate with the time and effort expended on such operations.

It may be submitted that this effort could not have been made without interfering with operations elsewhere and that such a concentration as is suggested could not have been effected for this reason alone—apart from any difficulties connected with operating additional units within striking distance of the objective through lack of aerodromes. Such may have been the case. Nevertheless, the point is worth bearing in mind when we come to consider how best we can employ the forces at our disposal in order to effect the greatest injury to the enemy. The solution of the problem must be dictated by the particular circumstances presented; but without concentration our effort is likely to prove fruitless.

Furthermore, we may draw the analogy of the submarines operating against merchant shipping. Aircraft, like the submarine, look for fruitful areas in which to concentrate their attacks. It is within these fruitful areas also that the defence will be found strongest and where, therefore, we may expect to find the enemy's aircraft. Greater concentration of effort will therefore be necessary if we are to achieve our object, for, before we are able to push home our attacks, the enemy's aircraft must be beaten.

One further important point that must be borne in mind is the fact that concentration is limited by the number of aerodromes that are available and situated within economic distance of our objectives.

To summarize, all our efforts must be concentrated in the first instance with the purpose of preventing the enemy from executing his plans. This will not only rob him of the initiative, but compel him to adopt a defensive policy. Only by the adoption of an offensive policy and by a concentration of our forces can this object be achieved.

(3) PRINCIPLE OF SURPRISE.

Surprise is the most effective and powerful weapon of war. To deceive the enemy, we must act with such rapidity and decision as to ensure that he will be ill-prepared to meet the stroke, and so will be forced to give way and conform to our movements. The rapidity with which aircraft can strike a blow, together with its range of action, give it enormous advantages, hitherto unpossessed by any arm, in carrying out both strategical and tactical surprise. Its ability to traverse wide areas confers on it the initiative to strike at will, when and in what direction it likes. This initiative is necessarily of very great importance, and the uncertainty as to where the next blow will fall makes it difficult for an enemy to devise plans to meet all contingencies. The importance, therefore, of gaining this initiative from the outset cannot be too strongly emphasized, for it constitutes the only effective method by which we can hope to safeguard ourselves against surprise and to force our opponent to fight at a disadvantage or conform to our movements. Instances of this, and the power of surprise possessed by aircraft, were of frequent occurrence during the late war, but, studied in the light of post-war developments, they furnish only trivial examples compared with present-day possibilities.

In an official narrative of the air activity prior to the Somme offensive of 1916, the following important paragraph appears: " It is a second great maxim of warfare [" Concentration " is here assumed to be the first] that surprise is an essential element of success. Now the air is conquered it has, to a great extent, opened to the gaze of the airman all the movements of an enemy, and, given Air Superiority, has rendered surprise in warfare more difficult. On the other hand, the air arm is itself capable of complete surprise. A sudden concentration of aeroplanes may take place along a given area in a very short space of time."

This is borne out in the following despatch from the Commander-in-Chief, British Forces in France, covering the operations on the Cambrai front, November, 1917:—

" No steadily advancing barrage gave warning of the approach of the German assault columns, whose secret assembly was assisted by the many deep folds and hollows typical of the chalk formation, and shielded from observation from the air by an early morning mist. *Only when the attack was upon our infantry great numbers of low-flying German aeroplanes* rained machine-gun fire upon them while an extensive use of smoke shells and bombs made it extremely difficult for our troops to see what was happening in other parts of the battlefield or to follow the movements of the enemy." Subsequent reports go to show that the Germans had made a concentration of flying squadrons in the battle area.

(4) PRINCIPLE OF ECONOMY OF FORCE.

The principle of economy of force is one which may be found difficult to apply. " To economise strength while compelling a dissipation of that of the enemy " requires on the part of a commander most careful thought and detailed study of each particular situation. Where economy of force is practised, we invariably find it applied *at the wrong time and place*. If we are to apply this principle correctly, it must be remembered that it involves " the correct distribution and employment of all resources in order to develop their striking powers to the utmost." *Time and place* are all-important. To allow the time for wise action to pass, will be bitterly repented when one strives later under disheartening difficulties to do what could have been done with comparative facility at the right moment. It is easy to be wise after the event. Nine-tenths of wisdom is being wise in time.

This principle may appear to many to be in direct conflict with " concentration " and for that reason may be held responsible for many of the mistakes of the past. In most cases, it would seem that " concentration " has been the overpowering influence. In this connection, one must always remember that the principles of war are all inter-dependent and that success depends upon the correct application of all those principles and not any particular one.

In an official statement of the reasons which governed the decision to employ part of our air forces in an attack on Germany during the last year of the Great War, the following passage appears: " Once our Air Force is strong enough to hold and beat the German Air Force, the extra effort on the battle front of still further bombing and fighting the Germans in France would not turn defeat into victory. *Increasing the strength of an Arm beyond what is necessary to ensure the superiority of that Arm, generally means that the extra forces are not used to the best effect, but only to reduce the effort to be made by those already employed."*

This aptly illustrates the application of the principle, " Economy of Force." This principle must be constantly developed, and can only be developed if, as already stated, the direction of those forces is in one hand. Economy of force does not lay in the direction of specialization of forces nor their employment in some specific function or one particular task only.

(5) MAINTENANCE OF THE OBJECT.

Among the more important factors to be considered in forming plans are :—

Time, Space, Weather, Relative Strength and Moral, Training, Armament, Communications, and General Resources.

The first duty is to appreciate the course of action which will most rapidly influence the enemy in the desired direction. In addition, a careful study must be made of the temper and national characteristics of the enemy people, their resources and means of subsistence.

The choice of objective must be governed mainly by considerations of the relative results to be obtained from success. Objectives likely to lead most rapidly to decisive results should, as a rule, be selected. The relative probabilities of tactical success must receive full consideration, for a strategical plan which ignores the possibilities of tactical developments is foredoomed to failure.

Strategy is a simple art in theory. It is clear in itself that the first thing a strategist must get clearly in his mind is what is the objective—that is, what he means to strike at. He must not only time his blows well, but when he does strike to put all available force into it. He should not direct from it any force whatever unless he can thereby induce an enemy to direct a stronger force and so make him relatively weaker where he means to strike him. An enemy cannot be overthrown unless his armed forces are defeated, and these remain as heretofore the primary " objectives."

The defeat of the enemy's armed forces and the maintenance of the freedom of military and naval movement will, in a war of any magnitude, entail the employment and concentration of the whole of our air forces with this primary object in view.

In considering objectives, the first point we must bear in mind is how best we can use the forces at our disposal in bringing the utmost pressure to bear upon the hostile nation. These objectives will, no doubt, be dependent upon the naval and military situation, the size of the country and the nature of its industries, and whether it is to any great extent dependent upon sea communications for bringing the raw material or food into the country.

What, then, are the chief objectives for air forces? I think it will be agreed that they are: firstly, to defeat the opposing air forces in battle; secondly, to attack targets of military importance as circumstances dictate, in order to support the naval, army and air operations; and thirdly, to attack, with due regard to circumstances and to the military situation, vital points within the enemy's country.

It is not intended here to discuss the merits or demerits of attack upon specific targets, such as railway centres, shipping, ports and docks, canals, factories. The actual targets for attack are dependent upon the plan of campaign and also on the results that can be expected.

If the enemy's aerodromes cannot successfully be attacked, either on account of their inaccessibility or for the reason that they are too scattered or too well protected, and we are unable to bring his forces in the air to battle, it will be the primary duty of our forces to attack those targets within his territory that will ensure the furtherance of sea, land, and air operations and which the enemy by their very importance will be forced to defend, and thereby effect the dual purpose of destroying his power to carry on the war and of bringing his air forces to battle.

The choice of objective, then, can never be determined with any degree of accuracy beforehand. No hard and fast rules can be laid down as to what our objectives will be. They will depend on the widely-varying circumstances presented with each war. Nevertheless, we must always keep in mind the principle that our first and main object must be the armed forces of the enemy. The object of the blow and the direction in which it is struck will be governed by considerations as to whether success will lead to decisive results.

It will serve a useful purpose here if we turn for a moment to the air attacks undertaken on Germany. In this connection, we can best study the following statement taken from a despatch of Air Chief Marshal Sir Hugh Trenchard, which contains a full and concise summary both in regard to the object and the principles underlying these attacks. The more important passages are placed in *italics*:—

"It will be within your recollection that in the past I had referred to the necessity for equipping the B.E. Forces on the Western Front with sufficient aircraft to *hold and beat the German air forces on the Western Front*, that the bombing of Germany was a luxury till this had been accomplished, but that, once this had been accomplished, it became necessary to attack what I may call the German Army in Germany, and to strike at its most vital point, its sources of supply; and the Independent Force was formed with this object.

"The question I had to decide was how to use this Force in order to achieve the object, *i.e.*, the breakdown of the German Army in Germany, its Government, and the crippling of its sources of supply.

"The two main alternative schemes were, firstly, a sustained and continuous attack on one large centre after another until each centre was destroyed, and the industrial population largely dispersed to other towns; or alternatively, to attack as many of the large industrial centres as it was possible to reach with the machines at my disposal. I decided on the latter plan, for the following reasons : In the first place, it was not possible with the forces at my disposal to do sufficient damage to completely destroy the industrial centres in question. And, secondly, it must be remembered that, *even had the force been still larger, it would not have been practical to carry this out unless the War had lasted for at least another four or five years, owing to the limitations imposed on long-range bombing by the weather.*

" By attacking as many centres as could be reached, the moral effect was first of all very much greater, so no town felt safe, and it necessitated continued and thorough defensive measures on the part of the enemy to protect the many different localities over which my force was operating.

"*Before it was possible to attack Germany successfully it was necessary to attack the enemy's aerodromes heavily,* in order to prevent his attacking our aerodromes by night, and by destroying his machines to render his attacks by day less efficacious. I considered that it was probable during the Spring and early Summer of 1919 that at least half my force would be attacking the enemy's aerodromes, whilst the other half carried out attacks on long distance targets in Germany.

" Out of a total of 550 tons of bombs dropped between 6th June and 10th November, 1918, no less than $220\tfrac{1}{4}$ tons *were dropped on aerodromes. This large percentage was due to the necessity of preventing the enemy's bombing machines attacking our aerodromes and in order to destroy large numbers of the enemy's scouts on their aerodromes, as it was impracticable to deal with them on equal terms in the air.*

" I also had to decide which targets would have the

greatest effect in hastening the end of hostilities. I decided that railways were first in order of importance, and next in importance the blast furnaces.

"The reason for my decision was that the Germans were extremely short of rolling stock, and also some of the main railways feeding the German Army in the West passed close to our Front, and it was hoped that these communications could be seriously interfered with, and the rolling stock and trains carrying reinforcements or reliefs or munitions destroyed. They were also fairly easy to find at night.

"I chose blast furnaces for the second alternative targets, as they were also easy to find at night, although it was difficult to do any really serious damage to them owing to the smallness of the vital part of the works."

It was also necessary several times during the period the force operated, to carry out attacks on the enemy's communications in support of the operations of the Army. The principles in this narrative underlying the course of action appear significant and conclusive. Many points of direct and indirect importance to this particular branch of the subject will be found throughout the subsequent chapters of this book.

It will suffice here to tabulate what may be termed the " unlimited activities " of aircraft. They are :—

(1) Attack on the enemy's air forces in the air, on his aerodromes and carriers, aircraft factories and depots.

(2) Attack on land forces, the strategical and tactical centres of an army, on its communications and supplies.

(3) Attack on naval forces at sea or in harbour, naval dockyards and bases.

(4) Attack on merchant shipping and ports in support of economic blockade by naval forces.

(5) Attack on factories, ports, railways, etc., with the object of undermining the moral of the people.

These will be discussed fully in succeeding chapters. There are, however, four important points in connection with this branch of the subject which should be borne constantly in mind. One might almost class them as inviolate principles.

Firstly, air forces must not be whittled away on operations that are unlikely to attain a tactical or strategical success.

Secondly, that a decision in the air must be reached at the earliest opportunity and the enemy forced into a state of uncertainty and moral and physical inferiority, thus preventing his taking the initiative.

Thirdly, air forces should actively aid the Navy or the Army as circumstances dictate with the whole of its forces.

Fourthly, that attention must first be given to those objectives that have a direct military importance affecting the subsequent operations of our armed forces, and whatever the principal objective, it should always be such that its achievement is within the power of the forces at our disposal.

(6) DIVERSIONS.

German air attacks on England and our own air attacks on Germany (which are discussed at greater length elsewhere) were not primarily undertaken with the object of carrying out a diversion. The former case is, however, a good illustration of a diversionary operation and one that was attended with conspicuous success. A very small force of German aircraft immobilized a considerably greater number of British aircraft (and incidentally personnel and *matériel* for ground defences) and so prevented their employment in offensive operations in the decisive theatre of war.

Apart from this operation, the only case recorded during the war of a diversionary operation by aircraft occurred in Palestine in September, 1916. Although it was on a small scale, it serves to illustrate both the effectiveness and importance of such an operation, more especially when undertaken in cooperation with land or sea forces so as to enable the latter's operations to be effected as a surprise. The operation referred to was carried out by aircraft off El Arish, which had the effect of diverting the enemy's attention from our troops operating against Bir El Mazar. The latter operation came as a complete surprise to the Turks, whose aircraft were employed in dealing with our air forces operating off El Arish. In amphibious operations, diversionary attacks by aircraft will figure largely in the opening phases of combined operations undertaken against an enemy's coast prior to landing troops.

Attacks by aircraft on some point or points away from the area in which it is intended that a fleet or army is to operate may cause the enemy to keep away his aircraft from that area by forcing him to counter these attacks and by thus deceiving him in regard to our real intentions. By distracting his attention, the operations of the other services will be freed from air menace, and surprise will be possible.

E

CHAPTER IV.

THE PRINCIPAL OBJECTIVE OF AIR FORCES.

SUCCESS or failure in war depends ultimately upon many factors, but it is obvious that a decision will always be reached by the feeling of the community. There are many historical instances in which wars, in spite of very weak organization or inferiority in numbers or armament, have been prosecuted successfully as a direct result of the keen public sympathy and the national determination to win. Public opinion, through the modern Press, makes itself felt very strongly, and undoubtedly influences both the results of the war and the methods by which it is prosecuted. The late war, still fresh in our memory, was full of instances of this, and every belligerent country was affected in one way or another by public opinion. If, therefore, the force of public opinion as a factor in war is once realized, it becomes clear that any operations we may undertake, or any methods we may adopt, favourable or unfavourable to our plans, which are likely to influence the will of the enemy people, must figure largely in our strategy.

As a corollary it is the duty of a government and the people of a country to make themselves acquainted with these military operations and to consider them impartially. This can only be done if citizens are educated in the general principles which govern the successful employment of the fighting forces in war, and the various factors which are essential to its successful prosecution. In this way a useful and intelligent public opinion will be formed, which will itself have a moderating and restraining influence. A general realization of the duty of every citizen towards the state and the armed forces in times of war will thus reduce the risk that public opinion will exert itself in a manner detrimental to the successful prosecution of war. The service of the community must be the supreme motive of every man, whatever the nature of that service may be.

In his book, "The Direction of War," Major-Gen. Bird writes:—"The end of war is usually attained when one nation has been able to bring such pressure on another that public opinion obliges the government to sue for peace. This pressure has been most effectively exercised through the defeat of the enemy's armed forces." By this I take it he implies that the defeat of the armed forces *leaves the way clear for subsequent pressure,* and so their defeat is often, not always, the signal for submission before that pressure becomes effective.

A novel feature of air power, and one which is believed by some to hold out the greatest promise of effective action, is that war can *at once* be carried into the enemy's country.

This fact raises the question as to whether pressure sufficient to end a war can be brought to bear on the spirit of a population by means of raids against such objectives as railroads, factories, power stations, etc., with the object of dislocating the life of the community. So long as the power of effective retaliation is possessed by the enemy, and his forces remain undefeated, it is doubtful whether this is so, even if raids are pressed to the utmost.

Retaliation in its turn will produce measures of defence on the part of the enemy which will so relieve the pressure that the old principle will in all probability reassert itself—that the first step towards winning a war is to establish superiority over the enemy's armed forces.

From this we can pass to a study of the moral effect of air attacks. The question has been uppermost in the minds of everyone as the result of the experiences of the late war. It still is a feature of all journalism, public speeches and conversations bearing on the question of air warfare. Whilst not wishing to underestimate the powers that aircraft possess of inflicting moral damage, and it is admittedly great, I suggest strongly that this question has received too much prominence and has come to be regarded by many people as constituting the chief function of aircraft, to the detriment of the sounder common-sense principles of war. It may have resulted in doing some good in educating public opinion and in preparing them for what may be inevitable. But has it not lead to dangerous conclusions when it is applied to military considerations? Are we to act on the principle that the main function of air forces is to attack the enemy people and that this is the true objective of all air forces? It would indeed be very unwise to think so.

The whole doctrine of air warfare must be studied in the light of principles of war, and not from any one aspect of the question, however important it may appear to be. *The degree of success that may be expected from these attacks must depend in the first place on air superiority, on the strength and regularity with which attacks can be undertaken, on the country attacked, on the psychological aspect, and on economic considerations and the military situation presented at the time.*

In " Air Power and War Rights," by J. M. Spaight, the following passage appears : " It is because of the tremendous moral effect of air attacks that they are at once likely to be carried out against objectives in the heart of an enemy country *and to be effective in their purpose of breaking down the enemy's will to resist.*" The truth of this depends on the points raised in the previous paragraph. If the conditions are favourable for carrying out such attacks—that is to say, air superiority has been established over the enemy, which allows of attacks being carried out in strength, and the military situation permits of such attacks being undertaken without detriment to the main operations,—then no one will doubt their efficacy.

The writer seems to have fallen into the error of considering all wars as more or less standardized. It is therefore essential to point out once more that every war has a different character, dictated by circumstances, and what applies to one may not, and in truth does not, apply to another. The writer appears to have based his argument on one particular war, that between a Continental power and England. It is, however, questionable whether in this case attacks would succeed in their object.

Once a belligerent had determined on attacking the hostile nation as a means of bringing it to terms, this course would be followed largely to the exclusion of other objectives and would leave the enemy's armed forces unmolested from the air. Apart altogether from this aspect of the question, will not the combined efforts of the armed forces tend to prevent the contestants resorting to such measures, or at least preventing them from concentrating a sufficient force for the attainment of the object?

The same writer continues: "Conservation of energy prompts the employment of any instrument or method in the manner or at the point which will give the maximum results." This is a sound argument, with which there can be no grounds for quarrel. It is "in the manner or at the point which will give the maximum results" that strikes at the root of the problem. Is this point the civil population? And will it always give the maximum results which in the opinion of so many it is thought capable of giving?

Compared with other methods of war, these attacks on an enemy country appear to be of the simplest kind, which, if successful, would give results out of all proportion to the time and energy expended. In reading Field-Marshal Robertson's book, "Soldiers and Statesmen," I was struck by the wisdom contained in the following passage, which has, incidentally, a very distinct bearing on the particular points under discussion.

In dealing with the project of the Dardanelles Expedition, he says: "Mr. Balfour also dwelt on the advantages which would be derived from the attack, *if successful,* and concluded by saying that ' it was difficult to imagine a more helpful operation.'

(There was no need to emphasize the advantages, and by constantly dwelling upon them there was a danger of obscuring the only points really at issue, namely, *Was the operation likely to succeed, and what might be the consequences if it failed?*) The stress laid upon the unquestionable advantages which would accrue from success was so great that the disadvantages which would arise in the not improbable case of failure were insufficiently considered. The omission is a common and very natural one on the part of those who, from want of practical experience, do not realize the difficulties and uncertainties which attend operations of war, *even of the simplest kind.*" (The *italics* are mine.)

There are, I venture to suggest, very definite principles to be considered before we can attempt to arrive at a correct estimate of the value of an air attack on a country.

These principles appear to be threefold :—

Firstly : That our air superiority is such as to warrant the expenditure of force, or conversely, that our air superiority can be further assured by such an attack.

Secondly : That the employment of the forces on such an operation does not imperil the success of our air, sea or land operations. Or as a corollary, that such an attack ensures the furtherance of our air operations, and directly or indirectly supports the general strategic plan.

And thirdly : That the attack is capable of attaining at least a tactical success.

Two illustrations of this may suffice. It will be recalled that the economic blockade effected by Germany's submarine campaign reached at one period a point within measurable distance of success. Had aircraft reached the state of present-day development, and had Germany possessed a sufficient force of such aircraft, this moment might have been chosen for intensive bombing attacks on the chief ports and distributing centres. This attack, combined with the economic blockade, might reasonably have had far-reaching results.

As a further illustration we have only to turn to our own intensive bombing of Germany, the effect of which was far more pronounced, coming as it did at a time when Germany was feeling the effects of the economic blockade, exercised by our Navy, at a time, therefore, when the German moral was cracking. Other things being equal, it is not too much to say that to gain the same effect without the economic blockade, a far greater force must have been employed in both these cases, and the attacks must have been spread over a considerably greater period of time.

The science of bombing, and the effectiveness of bombs have, during subsequent years, been improved upon, but this improvement is not, I think, sufficiently great to alter the conclusions materially. But here again we must expect improved means of combating aircraft. The latest developments in fighting aircraft alone is sufficient evidence of this.

The military side of this question can be summed up as follows : The object of war is to impose one's will on the enemy. The only sure method of attaining this object lies in the first place in the defeat of the armed forces, air, naval and military. The question of how best to employ the forces at our disposal to attain the common purpose is one which circumstances alone can decide.

Let us consider further this aspect of the question—the rôle of the air arm—and whether it will not be sounder strategy to concentrate on the military object, *e.g.*, defeat of the enemy's armed forces. Here again Mr. Spaight must be quoted at length, for the opinions he expresses are in the main held by most writers on this subject, and again I must question their validity.

In the first place, he states that " In its power of ' direct action ' it will see a means, and an effective one, of attaining that end without resorting to the slow, costly, ineffective, murderous procedure of conducting a campaign or of bringing a hostile fleet to action.

" Having this power to overleap the enemy's defences

will aircraft consent to behave as if they had not? Will they be so obliging as to approve a convention that the correct and traditional objects of attack are the protecting *corps d'armée*, the sure shield of the fleet of the opposing state, and that only when these are destroyed may the fruits of victory be gathered? Will they not rather eliminate the processes of the historical mode of warfare and set themselves from the outset to the work of exerting that pressure to which battles are merely the preliminary?"

The power of "direct action" expressed in the quotation given has already been dealt with. The question which automatically comes to mind in this " power to overleap the enemy's defences " is this : Is aircraft any more impervious to measures of defence than sea or land forces? If in any great measure it is so, then his assumptions cannot be refuted.

But is this really so? A close study of the late war disproves it. Aircraft suffered appalling losses at the hands of the defence—and it can be said that at the close of the war the evolution of the single-seater fighter, together with other measures of defence, had reached such an effective state in defence that the losses inflicted on aircraft were becoming a very serious drain on the resources of all belligerents.

That being the case, can we ever rely on possessing sufficient strength to carry out such a continuous offensive as will be necessary to gain the success which is predicted? I have no doubt that this will not be so. The object of aircraft will be analogous to that of the sea and land forces—the defeat of the enemy's forces— the gaining of air superiority, without which no operations can attain successful results. The fighting for air superiority will be continuous, and it is a question as to whether either side will possess such marked air superiority as to be able of itself to accomplish the task of imposing the national will on the enemy.

The whole theory propounded in the quotation given has been based on the assumption that the air forces of one power will be able to ignore the forces of the other. The late war proved this to be fallacious, and the next war will prove that, no matter how great production is, no matter how improved the air arm, the object—" the enemy's air forces "—will be of primary consideration.*

Again, we read " But steadily and surely, of the three categories of objectives of Air Power—the armies or fleets of the enemy, the military objectives outside the operational zones of those armies and fleets, and the general mass of property in the enemy state—the last will tend more and more to replace the two former categories as the focus of attention from the air. Armies which dig themselves into lines of trenches, supported by successive lines so deep and strong as to make a real break-through an affair of appalling magnitude, fleets which shelter themselves behind harbour defences and minefields and venture wholeheartedly upon a major engagement only by a sort of mischance, will be left to wage their own war of attrition."

Apart altogether from the fact that the writer makes no allusion to the opposing forces and air defence generally, this exposition entirely ignores any fundamental changes in armies or navies that have taken place and always will do so. Will armies and navies not undergo some changes with the advance of time? There are already signs of revolutionary changes in both those services. The armies of the future will be vastly more mobile and highly mechanized and no such condition as the stalemate that is depicted is likely to be experienced again.

There is, however, one important question that must here be dealt with arising out of the above quotation. That fleets or armies " will be left to wage their own

* The number of guns, of greater calibre, which aircraft will be capable of carrying in the future will tend to increase the severity of air fighting. It follows that armed conflict between the opposing air forces will become far more effective in their purpose and alone capable of achieving the object of war.

war of attrition" is a statement that cannot be allowed to pass unchallenged. If independent action on the part of each service is to be the foundation of the strategic policy of the nation, it will lead to bitter and justifiable resentment. Co-operation between the three fighting services was a feature of all the sea, land and air operations in 1914-18, and towards the end of the war, when aircraft had become more highly developed, the necessity of still closer co-operation manifested itself.

Sir Walter Raleigh puts the case clearly when he writes: " All other arms, even ships of war themselves, in many of their uses, are subservient to the infantry. Man must live, and walk, and sleep on the surface of the earth, and then, in the few feet of soil that have been fertilized by contact with the air, he must grow his food. These are the permanent conditions, and they give the infantry [or, to be more exact, the land forces] its supremacy in war. A country that is conquered must be controlled and administered; a city that surrenders must be occupied. Battles can be won in the air or on the sea, and the mark of victory is this, that the patient infantry, military and civil, can then advance, to organize peace."

The sea and air forces pave the way for a victory on land and it is their business to assist the land forces to the utmost. " It would be an ill service," he writes, " to the men of the air force, and a foolish ambition, to try and raise them in consideration above the heads of the men whose servants and helpers they are."*

Continuing, Mr. Spaight says: " They (the other services) will have, no doubt, the assistance of the necessary ancillary aircraft, but one must contemplate in future wars the existence of ' marginal ' air forces which can be employed strategically."

The ability of the air arm to be employed strategically in no way minimizes the importance of adhering to the principle of co-operation but rather accentuates it. Fleets and armies both have their strategical functions

*War in the Air. Raleigh.

to perform, but close co-operation between the three is essential for the complete success of either. What, one may ask, will be the effect on either sea, land or air operations if the "necessary ancillary aircraft"—to which Mr. Spaight refers—have the greater portion of the enemy's air forces pitted against them? What is to be considered "necessary"? Nothing short of the whole of our strength, to be employed both strategically and tactically in defeating the enemy's armed forces—in other words, in seeking the military objective. If further proof were needed, we have only to turn to a passage that appears later in the same book. "Sir Frederick Sykes has pointed out that, as the result of the demands of the Army and Navy for aircraft for directly military purposes, it was only in 1918 that 'we managed to secure a margin and formed the Independent Air Force in June.' . . . Even when the Independent Air Force was in being, it was still used to a great extent for attacking aerodromes close to the Front."

We can deduce from this statement that the military objective was still the main consideration in the councils of war.

Of still greater value as a proof of this is the footnote on the same page, which confirms the opinion already expressed. It is a statement made by Mr. Bonar Law in the House of Commons on October 16th, 1917: "There is no change of policy. It is our intention to employ our aeroplanes in Germany and over German towns *so far as the military needs render them free.*" Again, an official statement, published in *The Times* of October 1st, 1917, had stated already that the fact that no bombing raids were being carried out upon German towns was due "not to any reluctance to raid the enemy's towns, but to the *military* exigencies of the times."

These statements show quite clearly that the military needs held primary place. "Military" as here used must be taken in its broadest sense. It will not avail us to shut our eyes to this fact and to imagine that there will be less necessity in the future for concentrating on the military needs. Those needs are likely to make as heavy demands on the air forces as they did then, and only when they have been fully met will it be sound policy to devote the surplus forces to operations such as those described earlier; even then, it is questionable whether that policy would be a correct one. In any case, such attacks would have to be of such strength as to give reasonable chances of gaining a complete success, or a success so complete as to affect the strategic purpose; otherwise, at most they would have the effect of creating a diversion.

We must also remember that the combined forces of England and France, augmented in 1918 by American squadrons, were opposed to the single German force. This is not without its significance in considering the question and would seem to emphasize two points: firstly, the preponderance in aircraft that is necessary to ensure successful air operations and to gain air superiority; and secondly, how great a force was employed in support of the military operations.*

No nation will commence war with the amount of material we possessed at the end of four years of the late war, and it is in the question of quantity that we must limit our ideas.

It is over the principle in regard to the employment of aircraft that we are at variance with the writer, as also with the fact which is relegated to the background by those who seek to assure us of the success of such measures, that for this operation to succeed the opposing air forces would first have to be defeated or be in such inferiority that the defensive measures would not be equal to the task of preventing the enemy from gaining his object. This neither modifies the gravity of the air peril nor reduces the necessity of powerful air forces.

To sum up, there is no better refutation of such a doctrine than that given by the late Sir Cyprian Bridge,

*At the end of the war, Britain possessed 22,000 aircraft, France 20,000, and Germany about 18,000.

who, speaking on the question of "Victory by moral effect," said, "Opposed to this attitude is the very general conviction of mankind based on the records of nearly thirty centuries of belligerent procedure, that victory in war can be gained only by fighting for it, in or on whatever element hostilities may be conducted." In other words, victory is assured only when the fighting forces are defeated.

The moral effect of the raids undertaken during the late war was found to depend not so much on actual damage or casualties caused as "on the success or ill-success of the defensive measures." This is clearly borne out by evidence. It can be said that raiding and defence grew up together and when the latter had been adequately equipped and organized it proved successful.

The potentialities of this new technical invention were little known in the early stages of the war, and against them no defence had been prepared. The absence of this quite naturally left in the minds of the people a feeling of insecurity. Once the defence measures had been installed, the effect of raids on the moral of the people was greatly reduced.

The air offensive in France, coupled with the increased efficiency both in aircraft and ground defences, forced the Germans to abandon day attacks. During the few months of night attacks on our island, the barrage searchlights and guns and fast scouting craft prevented the majority of enemy machines from reaching their objectives. Out of a total of 118 enemy machines that were sent over during the months September-December, 1917, only 31 are reported as having penetrated the defences around London, *i.e.*, approximately 25 per cent. of the forces engaged. Statistics, it is said, can be made to prove anything, but the figures here quoted are, I think, quite significant.

In support of this contention, the following statement is to be found in the Official History of the War, dealing with Home Defence: "The last aeroplane raid on London took place on the night of 19th/20th May. By that time the success achieved by our machines had conclusively proved to the enemy that the night flying aeroplane, assisted by a well-directed searchlight scheme, was an effective counter to the night bombing aeroplane. It is safe to say that had the enemy made an attack on London between 20th May and 11th November, 1918, he would have suffered loss out of all proportion to the results he would have attained."

Again, it is to be noted that the success attained in 1918 by the air defences in France was even greater. Within a short period, no fewer than twenty-six enemy machines were brought down at night, which had the effect of putting an end to the enemy's air activity in that area. Defence well organized and equipped was therefore found equal to the task, and the attack could no longer be pursued without serious casualties.

In the middle of 1917, Admiral Bacon refers " to the necessity for command of the air during military operations," and says that this was becoming more manifest daily, so that the more efficiently we maintained and increased our air force on the fighting front, the greater the inducement to the Germans to devote their aircraft building capacity to supplying fighting machines for the army, and to consider seriously whether their constructional energies were, or were not, being wasted in building machines to drop bombs promiscuously on England. " Without doubt," he says, " so long as a surplus of aircraft supply existed, eccentricities such as attacks on London could be permitted by the military authorities; but when the pinch of supply came, then war necessities were certain to stifle the clamourings of the crank in support of useless but showy operations. Raids on England, therefore, about this time were largely on the wane."

It is interesting to note that the last two years of the war saw an increased necessity for a greater proportion of fighting aircraft. It was more and more realized that it was by this type that the maintenance of air superiority could alone be assured and that without it other types could not carry out their duties successfully. The increase in numbers of this type was common to all belligerents. General Ludendorff emphasizes this in his book, " My War Memories," and in a review of the German plans for 1917 he says that to increase the chaser squadrons was the most important thing. The failure on the part of the Germans to press home their attacks on London may be attributed in the first place to our offensive operations in France, and in the second to the efficiency of our organized air defence, which owing to lack of means had taken nearly four years to mature. Field-Marshal Sir William Robertson, in his book, " From Private to Field-Marshal," writes : " The loss of life and damage to property were however resolutely accepted, and instead of causing a panic and despair they made the people more determined than ever to see the War through to a finish. Thus, again, had the enemy mistaken the psychology of his opponent."

Field-Marshal Sir William Robertson proceeds to say that " the ostensible object of raids of this kind may be to inflict damage upon naval bases, supply depots, and other military establishments, but non-military places will also suffer, for although raids on them may theoretically be classed as unjustifiable the limits of what is permissible and what is not are very elastic in these days. Modern war being largely a matter of war against economic life, it has turned more and more towards the enemy's home country, *and the old principle of making war only against armies and navies has been consigned to the background.* Raids on non-military places and people may be regarded as barbaric, and they may, by exasperating the inhabitants, *have the opposite effect to that intended—the breaking down of the country's morale*—but they are bound to play a prominent part in the next contest, and on a far more extensive scale than in the late war." Here again I note that the author's statement contains no mention of war being waged against the opposing enemy air forces, and I must repeat the contention that the first and last war in which aircraft were extensively engaged proved beyond doubt that before any success could be attained superiority in the air had first to be gained and subsequently maintained.

In these days it is as well to remember that wars, however small, do not concern the belligerent nations alone. There is no country in the world that is not sooner or later affected in some way or another. The nations of the world as a whole have become interdependent, and this community of interest is now taking shape in the Councils of the League of Nations. It is not intended to imply that the League of Nations or any similar league will be able to control the destinies of the world at large or even influence the wills of nations. All it is intended to show is that a nation's actions in peace and war will be subjected to closer scrutiny on the part of those nations that are not direct parties to the dispute. Whereas few countries have ever maintained a navy large enough to make its weight felt in the event of their entering the struggle on one side or the other, and as in some cases geographical position has prevented their countries from assisting actively in a land campaign on the side they would wish, it must not be forgotten that all countries will possess air forces in sufficient numbers to assist materially in air operations and that geographical considerations in most cases will not prevent their employment in the particular theatre of war where they are required.

I am aware that this is a subject of very great controversy and that there are strong arguments in support of the use of gas, the bombing of towns and other equally terrifying forms of warfare. Nevertheless, we must not forget that the means of waging war does not, happily, rest with sailor, soldier or airman. Public opinion is the deciding factor and as such will restrict the use to which these new weapons will be employed. This may appear to many to be both short-sighted and fallacious, the words of a mere pacifist or idealist. I claim to be neither. If killing is not confined to the armed forces, then I hold civilization is doomed.

The popular idea that in the next war both belligerents will open air attacks on the enemy's capital and chief cities is founded on a misconception of strategy. If a nation is lured by this apparent short-cut to victory and neglects the true strategic objective in favour of bombing cities, it must leave its enemy's air, naval and land forces comparatively unmolested whilst opening out his own air forces to destruction and leaving his fleet and armies unprotected.

The following conclusions can therefore be safely drawn:—

(1) That raids should be confined to points of vital importance to the enemy and must conform to the general strategic war plan. Operations in support of naval and military forces will be of primary importance. If the situation is such that the defeat of the enemy's armed forces can be furthered by moral attacks and the air forces at our disposal are sufficient to gain their object, then and then only will it appear that such operations are warranted.

(2) Raids may be undertaken with a view to forcing a superior enemy to carry out a dispersion of his forces.

(3) Raids may be undertaken in support of an economic blockade.

In this last case, two alternative plans are presented. Firstly, in the case where the moral effects of the blockade have not yet made themselves felt, the targets for air attack will lie in the enemy ports, successful attacks on which would effectively hasten the gaining of the object. Secondly, where the moral effect of the blockade has once begun to assert itself, aircraft attack on the enemy country will have every chance of success.

To conclude, " Nations resemble individuals, and when at war wish to hurt the enemy with the least disadvantage to themselves. This will not be effected, nor will security be attained, if both sides mutually rush off to attack one another's towns, factories, harbours and other things or places that provide for the ordinary requirements of civilised life; and although both populations may suffer severely, the political aim, also, is not likely to be achieved unless one can win the race and quite outstrip the other in the work of causing misery, pain and death. But, if both sides, as is surely more natural, try to gain security by attacking the forces through which destruction can be carried out and fear caused, victory by one or the other may result, indeed has generally resulted, both in the attainment of the political aims and in security, that is, in avoiding damage to, or the annihilation of, civil amenities. The destruction of the enemy's armed forces has usually, therefore, in the past been the main strategical object, and it is, I think, likely to be the same in the future. If so, direct attack on a population will probably not be made unless one side possesses great preponderance of force in the air; or as a desperate attempt either to snatch success, or to stave off irretrievable disaster, by the nation whose armed forces are being defeated."*

This part of the subject has been dealt with at considerable length on account of its very great importance. I do not wish in any way to under-estimate the moral effects of air bombardment or to belittle the powers possessed by aircraft. Both are admittedly great. But however great they may be, they must not be allowed to carry our imagination to extremes or to lead us to believe that the air arm is the individual and all-powerful arm of the future. Let us study air power in the light of facts and with an unbiased and disciplined mind. The outward conditions determining war do not change by leaps and bounds, but do so gradually. Even the most momentous inventions—into which category aircraft certainly fall—do not suddenly produce a change of the factors influencing war. The fundamental principles of war remain the same, whether it is waged

*The Army Quarterly, January, 1926. Major-General Sir W. D. Bird.

on sea or on land or in the air. In order to achieve their object, whatever this may be, the first essential is to gain air superiority, and this can only be achieved by hard and continuous fighting.

INTRODUCTORY TO COMBINED OPERATIONS.
CO-OPERATION.

"In considering the future of the Navy it is impossibe to ignore aircraft. There are many important problems which the Navy and Air Service ought to work out together."—*The Crisis of the Naval War*, Admiral Viscount Jellicoe.

" An intelligent understanding of ' the other man's job ' is the first essential of successful co-operation."—Despatch dated March 21st, 1919, from Field-Marshal Sir Douglas Haig.

" Whatever the future may show that the Air Force is capable of doing in its independent capacity, it cannot be doubted that it will always be called upon to work in close and intimate co-operation with the Navy and Army."—"Aspects of Service Aviation," by Air-Marshal Sir H. M. Trenchard, *The Army Quarterly*, April, 1921.

" Aircraft are becoming more and more an indispensable factor in combined operations."—Field-Marshal Sir John French, June, 1915.

In any combined operation, it is essential to remember that success can only be gained by a resolute co-operation of all arms of the services in achieving the common object, and that object must always be kept foremost in the minds of all in considering the plan of campaign. If the mind is allowed to diverge from this fundamental principle, the only effect will be to make co-operation impossible. The danger lies, as history has so often proved, in commanders considering the problem only from their own and not essentially from the combined point of view. And the reason for this failure in the past has been that commanders have not always been able to appreciate either the true functions of their own particular service and its limitations, or even more those of the other services with which they have been called upon to co-operate. It is more essential than ever that not only commanders, but their subordinates should have a thorough knowledge of the functions of all three services, for without this knowledge co-operation or complete understanding cannot be achieved, and without this no combined operation can be successful.

The necessity of co-ordinating the work of the three services has long been recognized. Without such co-ordination, co-operation cannot be attained. The latter depends on the former for its existence.

The subject of co-ordination is constantly being discussed and suggestions are put forward from time to time in regard to the methods by which it can best be attained.

The hasty methods adopted in time of war to attain co-ordination cannot be said to have been entirely successful. What are the main reasons for failure? What are the difficulties with which we have to contend? The root cause of the trouble may be said to be the inherent difficulty that sailors, soldiers and airmen alike experience in casting their vested interests aside and looking at the problem from three sides instead of from only one.

In preparing for war and during war, everything must be done that is conducive to the success of the operations as a whole. Each service must make every endeavour to avoid anything in the nature of advancing its own interests to the detriment of the others, for this can never give success in battle, in which it is essential that all effort shall be subordinated to the common cause.

There is little doubt that the more each arm knows of the others, the more easily will co-operation be effected. If this is true of the arms of each service, it is surely even more true of co-operation between the three services.

What has been known previously as amphibious warfare, or the combined operations of fleets and armies, must now be known as warfare in three elements. The influence of aircraft upon the combined operations of fleets and armies necessitates a revision of thought in this respect.

CHAPTER V.

THE INFLUENCE OF AIR POWER ON SEA WARFARE.

I HAVE seen the following statement alluded to frequently in articles dealing with the combined naval and air problem.

"Acceptance of the air peril in no way modifies the gravity of the naval peril—that is, that the defeat of the British Fleet would inevitably mean the starvation of these islands, including, moreover, the complete inability of our Air Force itself to operate owing to the stoppage of essential supplies."

No one will dispute the truth of this statement, but it would be dangerous to leave the argument where it stands. We might with advantage add the corollary that acceptance of the naval peril in no way modifies the gravity of the air peril. That is, that the defeat of the British air forces would inevitably mean air attack on this country and its communications, and the complete inability of our fleet to prevent it. This is not to belittle the truth of the original statement, but to show quite conclusively that the two problems are of equal importance to the future security of this country and the Empire as a whole. The air peril presented at the moment may be a purely local one affecting Great Britain alone, but undoubtedly it will develop into one of general application affecting the Empire as a whole.

In the past, the commercial prosperity of England has been due to our insularity and the possession of the most powerful navy. To-day it must be realized that our very existence as an island power and the safety of our trade routes are dependent to an ever-increasing degree upon the maintenance of a powerful air fleet. Such a navy without such an air force will not suffice to safeguard our interests. Let us remember that for a century many countries have possessed no navy at all, while no single country has possessed a fleet sufficiently strong to challenge our naval superiority, whereas every country will now possess aircraft. And while, in the case of navies, some years must elapse before a sea force can be built of sufficient strength to disturb the balance of power at sea, it is possible to-day for any country to become a strong opponent in the air within a relatively short time.

Although aircraft were used with great effect during the late war in land operations, they were not utilized to anything like the same extent in naval warfare. This was due mainly to the fact that aircraft carriers were undeveloped and that the seaplane and flying-boat were but in their infancy. The radius of action of land 'planes prevented their useful employment with the Fleet when working from shore bases. The attacking power of aircraft against ships (with the exception of the submarine, against which aircraft proved of very great value) was also in the stage of early development.

Aircraft had, therefore, few opportunities, other than coastal reconnaissance, of exercising any serious influence upon the conduct of sea operations, and there was no real test to determine their powers of offence.

Progress since the war has been made both in armament and methods of attack, in addition to a general improvement in design and performance of all types of heavier-than-air craft. It is more particularly in the development of the flying-boat that improvement is most noticeable. The importance of this type to our Empire and its relative advantages over other types is dealt with elsewhere.

"We English," wrote Nelson in 1796, "have to regret that we cannot always decide the fate of the Empire on the sea." To-day we have to consider whether the fate of the Empire may not be decided by the combined powers of the sea and air. There are few who do not realize what air power means to this country and the Empire, and how vulnerable it is to air attack. We have also learned by bitter experience the power now possessed by the submarine and mine, and how these weapons nearly succeeded in bringing economic pressure to bear to the point of our submission. The results which could be attained by a combined effort of naval economic pressure and aircraft attack have yet to be demonstrated, but there can be little doubt that a combination of these two methods of waging war has enormous possibilities in the future.

We must remember that to-day practically no nation is self-contained and all nations are becoming more and more dependent upon supplies of food and raw materials from outside sources; if we bear this fact in mind, we see that economic factors are likely to play an increasing part in wars of the future. The power possessed by aircraft of attacking ships at sea, and perhaps that which is of greater importance, of effectively attacking ports and docks, increases the danger of economic pressure.

This fact alone is of considerable importance, and if we also take into account the extent to which aircraft can further affect that pressure by attacking inland centres of production and distribution, we can, without in any way over-estimating the case, come to the conclusion that sea and air power combined may be capable of reaching a far more rapid decision than heretofore, and likely to play the leading part in future wars. Thus we see that the fate of our Empire may well " be decided by sea and air power."

In sea warfare the fleet exists so that in war the control of the sea communications which we require may be secured. We require that control in order that:

We can attack the enemy's trade;

We can carry out combined operations;

We can make our own trade routes secure;

We can deny to the enemy routes which he may desire to control for overseas operations.

The best method of ensuring this control is to destroy all enemy naval forces which can dispute it.

The importance of this subject to Great Britain and the Empire is greater perhaps than to any other maritime nation, on account of their very livelihood being bound up in overseas trade. In war, as in peace, we have to procure the minimum requirements of life, food, clothing and fuel. Further, in war we cannot fight without an abundant supply of all war *matériel*, which again depends on industry and commerce.

Although the sailor's interests as opposed to the soldier's have remained deeper and more specialized in economic activities for the reason that during a war it is his business to make it possible to carry on the country's trade and to *prevent* the enemy carrying on his, that interest must now be shared in a great and ever-increasing proportion by the airman. The more fully, therefore, we understand this machinery of trade, the more effective will be our plans in protecting it.

There is one fundamental economic fact which may easily be lost sight of, and that is the necessity of keeping all trade routes open in war. We can only find safety in maintaining sea-borne trade, and this being so, we must be prepared to protect our sea communications with all countries. It has already been shown that there are very important parts of our sea communications which even to-day can be seriously threatened by aircraft attack. Thus we shall be confronted in the future with a new weapon capable of increasing the economic pressure. Moreover, the extent to which this menace may increase depends on the vitality of ships in ports and of the ports themselves. The ports and the ships within them offer an extremely vulnerable target to air attack, and it is not too much to say that any such adventure carried out on a large scale will probably necessitate the closing of the ports jeopardized. One port cannot be substituted for another, inasmuch as all ports cannot receive ships of the same size; each is equipped to deal with particular classes of goods and a certain volume of traffic, while each is designed to serve a particular area and cannot easily distribute goods in a wider zone. From these facts alone, it will be seen that the disabling of even one port will cause very serious disorganization.

The effect of the submarine attack is fresh within our memories. What might conceivably happen in the case of such an attack in close combination with a simultaneous attack by aircraft, on even one of our great ports —rendered more effective by the congestion of shipping and goods—will scarcely bear reflection.

The importance of this subject to a country dependent upon its overseas commerce is obvious, and everything must be done to afford aircraft protection in those areas open to attack from the air.

History has shown that it has always been a most difficult task for a superior naval force to impose its will upon a weaker naval adversary who, by keeping his battle fleet in positions of safety in fortified harbours, where they are a constant threat to the sea communications of the stronger naval power, imposes upon the latter a watching policy.

The situation here indicated is interesting since the advent of aircraft, for in this new weapon we possess the means of attacking the enemy fleet. By an attack on the port or ports by aircraft, the enemy fleet can be harassed constantly and even if it does not suffer very great material damage, the loss of fighting efficiency from the moral effects of such attacks will be an important factor, and conceivably might force a fleet into a position of less strategic value.

In the foregoing paragraphs of this branch of the subject, I do not wish it to be inferred that aircraft will in the future supersede the Navy in sea warfare. The aeroplane, like the submarine, destroyer and mine, has merely added to the dangers as well as to the effectiveness of sea warfare. Aircraft have added to the complexity of naval warfare, and may well change the application of the principles of naval strategy.

Though we have, in the new air arm, a weapon which presents unique possibilities, yet at the present stage of its development we must not fall into the error of imagining that a too sudden and overwhelming change will take place as a result of the introduction of this new arm into warfare.

That the Navy must receive ample air support if it is ever to carry out its functions in future is an accepted fact. From this we can pass to a more detailed study of the functions of aircraft in sea warfare. They are principally the following :—

(a) Offensive action against hostile aircraft and protection of our fleet from air attack.
(b) Reconnaissance.
(c) Bombing attacks on naval ports and ships in harbour.
(d) Bombing and torpedo attacks on ships at sea.
(e) Operations in support of a military landing.

(a) *Offensive Action against Hostile Aircraft.*

This must be considered the first duty of aircraft. Every endeavour must be made to gain superiority in the air, by the judicious use of offensive patrols and by bombing attacks on his air bases and carriers. Such attacks must be relentless in character and everything must be done to prevent the access of his aircraft to our own coast line or bases of operation. His air arm must be thrown on the defensive and the initiative denied him.

(b) *Reconnaissance.*

The ability of aircraft to search sea areas and to locate naval vessels operating in such areas has materially assisted towards the solution of one of the most arduous and difficult duties which have been the lot of certain naval vessels.

The difficulty of patrol vessels, even in the North Sea, which is a comparatively small area, in locating or intercepting enemy vessels, was manifest during the war. It was recognized that a watch could only be maintained on a very limited area at one time. To have kept the whole of the North Sea under observation would have necessitated the employment of a prohibitive number of patrol vessels, for the effective distance of observation from a vessel in the North Sea under normal conditions during the day is only nine miles. The evasion of patrol vessels by the enemy was therefore a comparatively simple matter and a constant source of anxiety, and it forced our fleet to adopt certain dispositions which would not otherwise have been necessary.

Reconnoitring patrols of aircraft will be established on the outbreak of war, and the opposing enemy forces will be kept constantly in view from the air and the enemy's movements will be reported.

The fleet's work and dispositions will be dependent upon aircraft reconnaissance. Whereas in the past naval units have had to be detached to carry out raids on the enemy's outlying bases to ascertain the strength of such forces, aircraft will now prove an effective and better means of ascertaining such information.

The danger of raids on the East Coast by German naval forces led to a division of the fleet, with its attendant disadvantages from the strategic point of view. In the future, enemy naval forces will be unable to carry out such raids with the same security (except in conditions of weather unfavourable to aircraft), for their movements will be subject to detection and report by aircraft and they will be engaged by aircraft based on shore. The lack of information as to the movements of the enemy fleet throughout the war was a factor of considerable influence in naval strategy. The importance of aircraft reconnaissance to the fleet, therefore, cannot be over-estimated. Had our fleet been able to keep an effective look-out off the enemy ports and to obtain warning of the sailing of enemy ships, the difficulties experienced and the risks forced upon it would not have been nearly so great. The speed and range of aircraft are factors which make them especially valuable as a means of gaining information. Further development will increase their powers in this respect.

The difficulty of obtaining information throughout the whole Battle of Jutland was most pronounced. Information regarding the position of hostile vessels was often received too late for successful action to be taken. Instances are afforded of the valuable assistance rendered to the High Seas Fleet on occasions such as the warning by Zeppelin scouts of the approach of the Grand Fleet on August 19th, 1916, when a portion of the former fleet had left its bases with the apparent object of carrying out a raid on our coasts. In future, during daylight and subject to weather conditions, all movements of a fleet will be known through the agency of aircraft. Contact between the two opposing fleets will not therefore be a matter of chance. *It will only be brought about by deliberate action on the part of both sides to force a battle.*

When the two opposing fleets have once closed for battle, every movement will be observed by aircraft and reported. It will be a difficult matter for a fleet to extricate itself from an engagement except under cover of darkness and unfavourable weather conditions preventing air operations.

One of the most far-reaching effects on future naval operations is the fact that concealment and evasion will be practically impossible during daylight (in fact, in all cases where more than eight hours are required for concentration). We witnessed during the late war the difficulties presented in this respect. Apart from the fact that the German Fleet did not wish to fight, the ease with which it was able to evade our forces demonstrated the need for some new means by which to ensure earlier and timely information regarding the movements of that fleet, and also greater certainty of keeping in touch with it once it was sighted. This grave disadvantage will disappear to a great extent now that aircraft has reached a high state of development, and it is therefore probable that future fleet actions will be fought to more decisive conclusions.

One other important consideration is the probability

of a radical change in fighting tactics as a result of the use of aircraft. There is already a distinct possibility that the stereotyped formations we saw employed during the actions referred to may be avoided or disappear altogether. In place of the line ahead we may see battleships employed fighting in divisions and coming to much closer grips with the enemy. This change in tactics will surely be possible with better and quicker information and with improved means of communication. This may to a certain extent presuppose a slight advantage in the matter of speed over the enemy. Nevertheless, it is one which should seriously be considered if we are ever to gain a decisive victory at sea in the future.

(c) *Bombing Attacks on Naval Bases, Docks and Ports.*

The greatest scope for aircraft in the future seems to lie in their power of rendering fleet bases uninhabitable to ships and personnel alike, and in the destruction of docks and all their necessary naval paraphernalia. Any base or port within reach of shore-based aircraft will be subjected to this form of attack. A fleet is valueless without efficient and secure bases. One has only to turn to the Mediterranean to realize the importance of this fundamental fact. What, for instance, would be the effect if both Gibraltar and Malta were so severely menaced by air attack as to render them useless to our fleet? The answer is, of course, that our fleet would have either to quit the Mediterranean or find further bases by which their position could be rendered less liable to attack from the air, and around which we could station sufficient air forces for their defence. Neither Malta nor Gibraltar can be regarded as secure from air attack, owing to their position and isolation, the latter of which renders them even more vulnerable owing to the limited numbers of land aircraft that can be operated from either of these places.

A further question which may very well be asked is— what will be the probable effects on the strategic dispositions of our fleet in case of war with a Continental power should the whole of our bases on the southern coast be open (as they most certainly will be) to constant air attack? The obvious answer is that our fleet will be forced to take up a position that cannot give it the same strategic advantages, with the result that it cannot exercise the same control over the essential sea communications, with the probable effect of surrendering the initiative to the enemy, or at least of giving the enemy greater liberty of movement.

In proof of this, it is useful to recall the effect of Zeebrugge and Ostend as bases for German light craft and submarines.

Again, the result of such bombardment of these bases from the air as was then possible was sufficient to prove that attacks, if carried out on an intensive scale, would have rendered them untenable.

Finally, to demonstrate still further the importance of this question, we have only to refer to the words of Admiral Mahan :

" In a naval war coast defence is the defensive factor, the Navy the offensive. Coast defence when adequate assures the Naval Commander-in-Chief that his base of operations—the dockyards, coal, and depots—is secure. It also relieves him and his Government, by the protection of commercial centres, of the necessity of considering them, and so leaves the offensive arm perfectly free."

In the offensive, then, bombing attacks on naval ports, docks, etc., will be among the most important rôles which aircraft will perform in support of the fleet. For such attacks to be successful, surprise or superiority in the air will be the first essential. Successful attacks on such targets may force the enemy to make other strategical dispositions, and his whole strategical plan of operations will be affected thereby.

The number and proximity of the enemy's bases, the length of his coast line, and the alternative strategical bases on which he can fall back in case of necessity are all points that have a direct bearing on these operations.

Air superiority and the resultant attacks on naval ports, etc., may have the effect of:—
(1) Wearing down an enemy's fighting efficiency by causing losses among his ships, docks and naval depots, etc.
(2) Causing him to change his strategical dispositions by denying him the use of those bases which are essential to his strategical plans.
(3) Forcing him to accept battle on disadvantageous terms.

These considerations will call for careful thought in the selection of future naval bases and dockyards. Not only must they be chosen from the point of view of maritime utility, but also from that of A.A. defence, and they must be so placed that their distance from likely hostile aircraft bases will render them less liable to serious attack.

An interesting extract from a minute written by Mr. Winston Churchill to the First Lord of the Admiralty in September, 1914, may be quoted as being of considerably greater importance to-day. He wrote: "There can be no question of defending London by artillery against air attack. It is quite impossible to cover so vast an area; and in London, why not every other city? Defence against aircraft by guns is limited absolutely to points of military value. . . . Far more important than London are the vulnerable points in the Medway, at Dover and Portsmouth. Oil tanks, power houses, lock gates, magazines . . . all require to have their A.A. defence increased. Portsmouth in particular requires attention now that enemy's territory has come so near.

"*But after all, the great defence against the air menace is to attack the enemy's aircraft as near as possible to their point of departure.*" The problem then confronting the First Sea Lord was comparatively small in comparison with the problem which confronts the nation to-day.

Important naval bases must therefore be secured

against air attack. Our air forces must not, however, be whittled away in purely passive defence of strategic positions. It will be impossible—as it happened with the Navy—to prevent raids at every point. Allusion is made elsewhere to the immense advantages to be gained by continual offensive operations in the air against enemy aircraft. By such means can the defence of positions be best maintained. When aircraft are relied upon for purely defensive operations, the demand will outstrip the supply available and will lead to a division of force.

Nevertheless, it appears essential that a well-organized defence consisting of fighter aircraft, A.A. guns and searchlights be available for the defence of vital points.

(d) Bombing and Torpedo Attacks.

How effective aircraft can be against various types of naval vessels has yet to be determined. Certain experiments have been made since 1918, but the reports available are somewhat meagre and leave one in an unhappy state of uncertainty. At all events, there seems to be little in the way of definite material on which to base satisfactory conclusions. It would appear from the published reports that the experiments determined that the projectiles used by aircraft are superior to the defensive features of construction of the vessels attacked. On the other hand, it is known that the vessels used as targets were obsolete in regard to their protective construction from torpedoes and bombs. During the war, the comparative ineffectiveness of the torpedo against battleships was proved beyond doubt. There is also the lack of any war experience in this form of attack by aircraft. The important question is whether we can logically anticipate that aircraft projectiles will be superior to the defensive construction of vessels. We are at present in the state of experimental knowledge, and such data as we possess undoubtedly induces us to the conclusion that, although the effectiveness of aircraft attack on vessels is at present not great, yet the further development of aircraft and aircraft projectiles will necessitate additional defensive armament of vessels, more especially, perhaps, against bombing. It is in this method of attack that greater development may be anticipated.

Recent developments of aircraft point favourably to the assumption that their offensive powers against vessels are increasing, but we have also to remember that the protective measures against this form of attack are also becoming more effective. Before attacks can be undertaken with success, air superiority must be assured in order that attacking 'planes may be able to carry out their mission unimpeded by enemy aircraft.

(e) Operations in support of a Landing.

As a result of aircraft development, invasion will become an even more hazardous proceeding than in the past. Control of the sea and sea communications have in the past been necessary to any force attempting invasion, and to this must now be added complete superiority in the air. Troop transports are particularly vulnerable targets for both torpedoes and bombing aircraft, and during the process of transporting troops across the sea and up to the time of disembarkation, the invading force must therefore have sufficient aircraft protection to ensure that no attack in force from hostile aircraft can be made against it. After disembarkation, a continual offensive action in the air must be undertaken to ensure the success and safety of the invading force, and to secure its bases and supplies from air attack.

The Dardanelles operations provide interesting study. What effect can we reasonably suppose would have been produced on these operations if air superiority could have been thrown into the scale?

Let us take the situation as it might have presented itself to either side. The Turkish forces in defence would have been in a position of great advantage from the point of view of aircraft bases, and in a position to concentrate the whole of their available forces within the area of operations. On the other hand, the Allies would have been at a great disadvantage in this respect, as no facilities existed for establishing air bases other than on the islands of Imbros, Tenedos and Lemnos. The distance of these bases from the objectives for air attack would have precluded any hope of relying upon the support essential to the operations as a whole.

Our armies could not have been landed in face of aircraft attack and could not have been maintained unless air superiority could have been established and continued. That is, the enemy air forces must have been defeated and thus prevented from seriously affecting both our landing and subsequent operations.

Let us consider, too, the problem of forcing the Straits by the fleet. No one will hesitate to confess that the initial operations conducted by the Navy could not have been attempted without air superiority, as the ships engaged in forcing the Straits would have been subjected to a heavy and continuous air attack; there could also be no question of our being able to utilize aircraft based on carriers, for the risk of air attack from the shore-based aircraft would have been a sufficient reason for deciding against such an undertaking.

From these facts alone it will be seen:—

Firstly, that air superiority will be an essential preliminary to the operations of either naval or military forces.

Secondly, that the maintenance of air superiority is essential to the success of subsequent operations.

Thirdly, that aircraft in the defence have made both naval and military operations which comprise a landing more difficult, and, in point of fact, impossible without complete air superiority or surprise.

Fourthly, that, given air superiority, it may be possible for such operations to be undertaken with a smaller expenditure of naval and military forces.

AIRCRAFT CARRIERS.

Aircraft carriers I believe to be a stop-gap, and in another ten years or even less they will have reverted to depot ships for flying-boats and seaplanes, fighting aircraft alone being carried on all the larger types of ships. A movable base may be considered to have its advantages, but these will be found to be unimportant when compared with the other issues involved. On a thorough investigation of the matter it becomes quite evident that the inherent limitations of the aircraft carrier as a base of operations for aircraft are unremediable and place upon aircraft additional restrictions under certain conditions. It also renders the aircraft immobile.

The chief limitations of the aircraft carrier are, firstly, its vulnerability to attack both from warships and aircraft; secondly, its inability to operate aircraft under all conditions of weather and therefore at the time and place desired. In this respect carrier-borne aircraft are at a very distinct disadvantage as compared with the flying boat or shore-based aircraft.

The inevitable difficulties of operating aircraft carriers in time of war cannot be generally appreciated or understood; and this is perhaps natural, seeing that they are a peace-time product. The flying boat has now definitely proved its general seaworthiness and reliability. It also possesses great powers of offence and defence. It has in addition a very wide range of action, and by utilizing the sea as its natural base of operations has its mobility unimpaired. This being so, there can be little doubt that for the price of even one aircraft carrier and its machines and the cost of maintenance, a whole fleet (a minimum of 150) flying boats could be kept in commission, the fighting value of the Navy greatly enhanced, and the control of the sea communications much simplified.

It must also be remembered that nearly every great naval battle of the past has been fought within a reasonable distance of the land; and the distance which a modern fleet can fight away from its base is limited, apart from the strategical disadvantages of fighting a sea battle many hundreds of miles from its base.

It is therefore logical to assume that not only flying boats, but shore-based aircraft, can be relied on in the future to take part in any fleet action. Aircraft for work at sea must be able to carry out their functions independently of their base, using the sea as their natural base from which to operate. *This alone will enable them to make full use of their mobility,* and will, in addition, increase their reliability for operating at sea and give them greater freedom of action.

Reference has been made to the efficacy of the flying-boat for work at sea. Its importance demands special and more detailed consideration. In this type we have the greatest chance to evolve the true ocean-going aircraft which can normally use the surface of the sea, but can take to the air when necessary.

Considerable improvement in the primary consideration—seaworthiness—has already been made; and we can say quite definitely that, in the latest type of boats, we have reached that stage in design where we have good all-round performance and a good " get-off " or landing in anything save very heavy seas.

For coastal patrol, present design affords us an eminently suitable boat which can operate independently of its base, provided that a sheltered anchorage is available. Already this has been proved practicable, with little outside assistance except refuelling.

Considerable advance is being made in performance, seaworthiness, and the protection of vital parts from sea-water and spray in the construction generally of metal hulls.

It is already a practical proposition for flying-boats to operate in conjunction with a parent ship, tender and dock. Mooring a boat out is less harmful than the continual lifting in and out of the water on trolleys necessary in the use of carriers, and in addition operations are more quickly performed. Moorings can be laid at which boats will lie safely.

Refuelling at sea in favourable weather is feasible. From flying-boat cruises it has been found practicable even on older types—even under bad weather conditions —to operate and maintain a self-contained unit of flying-boats at a distant base for a prolonged period with the minimum of spares and personnel. Sheltered anchorages are the only necessity, and these are not difficult to find.

Their employment in such waters as the Pacific and the Indian Oceans would be an invaluable asset to the fleet. The remarkable capabilities of these machines have been demonstrated during recent years both in this country and America. In both countries the flying-boat is receiving the attention it deserves, and many cruises have been undertaken to test their qualities in a manner which permits of no doubt regarding their existing and possible future capabilities.

As a further proof of their value, it is only necessary to refer to the many long-distance flights over the sea that these boats have accomplished during the past year. The further development of the type is of special importance to us as an Empire whose communications must always include long flights over seas.

AIRSHIPS.

This chapter would, I feel, be incomplete without reference to the airship, which, in my opinion, will prove capable of carrying out many of the more important functions which its most ardent and enthusiastic supporters contend to be possible of achievement.

In any case, they will be an important adjunct in the defence of our overseas communications. Their vulnerability both to gun fire and to attack by aeroplane is admitted, and accordingly their employment over hostile areas, at any rate in clear weather, cannot be considered. They could in any case only be adequately protected by a fighting force of aeroplanes up to the latter's extreme range. It would therefore be more economical and efficient to employ other forms of aircraft for offensive action.

That they have, even in their present state of development, very definite and useful functions cannot be denied, and with further experiments in design we may yet see the airship play an important rôle both in strategy and tactics.

In certain respects, airships are superior to other types of aircraft. They have a much larger carrying capacity, and a far greater radius of action, than any heavier-than-air machine yet designed. As far as can be foreseen, they will continue to hold their advantages in these respects. In addition, an airship has a longer range in wireless telegraphy, can be navigated far more easily in clouds, and in fog does not suffer the serious drawbacks of the heavier-than-air machine.

Another disadvantage of the airship which we must consider at the present time is its expense both in construction and maintenance. In view of this, it is probable that the money could be more advantageously employed in the development of large sea-going flying-boats.

Nevertheless, no empire nation can afford to neglect the airship on this score alone, but should give every encouragement, financial and otherwise, to the development of airships and to improvements in their design.

Their capacity for employment at night over vast stretches of sea (where there would be little risk of attack), suggests valuable uses in reconnaissance, and also great powers of attack on docks and harbours, provided they can reach their objective across sea and return during hours of darkness and that their attack can be carried out as a surprise.

But apart from these considerations, the airship has very limited powers as an offensive weapon, and its rôle in a future war will not be so much in the offence as in its utility as a more reliable and rapid means of locomotion for inter-communication, or as a means of carrying urgent stores and personnel, either in the way of officials or reserves for the fighting forces, over large distances.

The future importance of the airship may lie in its employment as an auxiliary to heavier-than-air craft in the conveyance of aircraft personnel, stores and equipment to far-distant bases, or in replenishing aircraft carriers at sea. With our widely-scattered Empire and the distances which must necessarily separate the scenes of operations from our main base of supply (England), the airship will prove a very important means of rapid transport.

To cite just one instance of this. We can take the case of our aircraft carriers being employed on some distant operation either in conjunction with a fleet in battle or in combined operations. After the first encounter with the opposing air forces, it may be important to repair the losses both in aircraft and personnel. If, as will be possible, the replenishment of these losses is rapid, it may have a very important effect upon the subsequent operations; in fact, it may easily mean the difference between victory and defeat in the air, and the success or failure of the whole operation. In the absence of this rapid form of transport, the reserves for the aircraft carriers would either have to be brought up by sea in another ship or they would have to return to its supply base.

It is already within the realms of possibility for aircraft to fly on and off an airship, and, although the numbers of such machines which an airship can carry are at present very limited, yet the question is of importance where the rapid conveyance of even a small number of them to the scene of action (such as during a fleet action) may have far-reaching consequences. If, for instance, it is found during a fleet action that insufficient fighters are available to maintain air superiority, the deficiency can be made good by bringing up reserves of this class of aircraft in airships.

By carrying their own defensive patrols of fighting aircraft, airships may be economically employed on reconnaissance duties up to what may be termed the "approach period," *i.e.*, before heavier-than-air craft can be utilized owing to the wide stretch of sea which they have to cover. Reconnaissance over such widespread waters as the Atlantic or Pacific would render their employment distinctly advantageous and would save the aeroplanes for their more legitimate work. *For searching large areas for commerce raiders or enemy submarines, they have also very definite economical advantages.

The rapidity with which heavier-than-air craft have been developed and the financial stringency operating since the war, has militated against the development of this type of aircraft. These reasons, however, do not justify neglecting to take the type into account in a study of the problems confronting us. It is important that due weight should be paid to their utility and future progress.

In his book, "The Crisis of the Naval War," Admiral Viscount Jellicoe asks the question, " What are we to do in the future to ensure the safety of the communications between these islands and the rest of the Empire?" He proceeds, " As a matter of course we should be in a position to safeguard them against any possible form of attack from whatever quarter it may come." He points out that " there is no possible chance, for at least a generation, of aircraft competing commercially with transport in vessels sailing on the sea. Therefore the problem of guarding our communications resolves itself into one of securing the safety of vessels which move upon the surface of the sea, whatever may be the character of the attack."

Whilst not entering into any discussion as to the method by which these vessels can be protected, he points out " that it is necessary for us to be in a position of superiority in all the weapons by which their safety may be endangered. At the present time," he says, " there are two principal forms of attack (1) by vessels which move on the surface, and (2) by vessels which move under water. A third danger—namely, one from the air, is also becoming of increasing importance. The

*These could be a smaller and faster type of airship.

War has shown us how to ensure safety against the first two forms of attack . . . " and he leaves the question of aircraft attack to be answered.

The war proved quite conclusively that the only efficient method of countering aircraft attack was with air forces, and there has been no recent development which would justify us in changing that opinion, nor is there ever any likelihood of an efficient substitute. Developments in this form of attack are making remarkable progress, and we may say quite conclusively that it is one to be reckoned with very seriously. Air attack on merchantmen at sea by torpedoes or bombs and attacks on ships in harbour or dock constitutes a grave menace.

Earl Jellicoe states a truism when he says that " there are many important problems which the Navy and Air Service ought to work out together." No one will deny the importance attached to this statement, but when he follows it with the sentence, " Air power is regarded by many officers of wide practical experience as an essential complement to sea power, whatever future the airship and aeroplane may have for independent action," it would seem to be carrying the argument into deep water.

A Fleet air arm may be essential to the fighting efficiency of a fleet so long as the aircraft carrier survives, and no one will deny that the control of such forces in operations with a fleet at sea must be vested in the Commander-in-Chief. But for air action proper, divided control of air forces means dispersion and the loss of fighting efficiency in the air.

The advent of aircraft has introduced new, and, at present, only partially-explored problems into naval warfare.

The importance of aircraft only accentuates the necessity of thinking in terms of air warfare whenever we are called upon to solve or elucidate a future naval problem. I have shown that aircraft will not only modify our naval tactics and construction, but will irresistibly exert an important influence also on naval strategy.

CHAPTER VI.

THE INFLUENCE OF AIR POWER ON LAND WARFARE.

It will be interesting first to study the probable effect of air forces on land strategy. During the late war, more especially in its last year, the air arm was beginning to affect the land operations to an extent which would ultimately have caused a revolution in the conduct of war on land. The relentless attacks carried out on depots, railways, and points of strategical and tactical importance behind the enemy's lines played an important part in preparing the enemy's overthrow (ending in his final and sudden retreat). In any future war these attacks are likely to be far more formidable, owing to the probable greater destructive power of aircraft, and a zone behind the enemy's lines of considerable depth relative to the length of the battle front will be rendered almost untenable. The position of the defending force will therefore be precarious. It is questionable whether under these conditions a land attack can ever be pushed to advantage unless the attackers have first obtained superiority in the air. We can assume, therefore, that, unless greater mobility and protection are afforded an army (measures in regard to which are discussed later), the air forces will occupy a position of paramount importance in the development of successful land operations, and will undoubtedly provide the first line of attack before the advance of the land forces. We might carry this line of thought a step further and say that it is within the power of the air arm to force the enemy to withdraw from a sector of its front, and so compel him to fight in an area of strategical disadvantage.

This is borne out by many instances which could be quoted of the operations on all fronts during the late war. In his book, "Die Schlachten im Sommer, 1918," General von Zwehl writes: " Of considerable moral as well as material effect on the German defence also were the masses of low-flying aeroplanes which took part everywhere in the fight with bombs and machine-gun fire."

An army's communications will in future be liable to destruction from the air, and this important point will necessitate (a) greater mobility, (b) a revision of its dependence upon railways and other equally vulnerable means of transportation for supply.

It follows, then, that land warfare must undergo some alteration in character. The power of defence will be greatly increased where superiority in the air is manifest. Without superiority in the air, the defence loses to a great extent the tactical advantage it holds. Again, the strategical advantage of the attack is diminished with the loss of superiority in the air.

Col. the Hon. M. A. Wingfield, in an article on " Air Operations against the Lines of Communication of an Army,"* discusses the relative advantages of air attacks on various points in the lines of communication of an army, and what definite influence on a battle might be exerted by such attacks directed against the enemy's administrative services rather than against his fighting troops. The conclusions he comes to may be summarized as follows:—

Firstly, the interference with an enemy's line of communication in rear of his bases would have a very delayed action at the front, when compared with similar interference in front of his bases.

In support of this judgment, he gives an example in the situation that existed in May, 1918, as it affected the British Second Army. This was "sufficient to show what a narrow margin of safety existed in the transportation services behind our front. The blocking of

The Army Quarterly. January, 1926.

the railway lines for six days would have emptied the entire echelons and reserves available at the front, and much less than this would have been sufficient to dislocate the whole system and prejudice the success of any operations in progress."

His conclusion is, therefore, that the danger spot of the whole administrative system appears to lie in front of an army's base, not behind it. This may be true where the transportation services are limited to a narrow margin of safety, as in the illustration cited. Similar circumstances may not infrequently occur until the cross-country tractor is developed, and there can be little doubt that when such conditions exist the attack should be made on that portion of the line of communication indicated.

Secondly, in considering further the point raised, the same writer proceeds " to determine what points in front of the base are most suitable for attack. This, again, requires a detailed study of a particular situation, and accurate knowledge, not only of the actual dispositions of the enemy's administrative arrangements, but also of the principles upon which his administrative machine works, before the most suitable targets for air attack can be chosen, and before it is possible to realise what actual effect can be produced."

With regard to an attack on the bases of an army, it is obviously expedient to make such an attack if there is only one available. An instance of this may be cited in the expedition based on Salonika, a sustained air attack on which would have placed the Army in this place in a precarious position.

Again, he emphasizes the important fact that, in this as in all operations, " to achieve success which is going to be anything like decisive, not only must heavy attacks be made on the right targets, but they must be kept up continuously for a considerable period," and, further, that with heavier bombs and greater accuracy, a decisive success may well be within the bounds of future possibility. " It is a subject," he says, " on which it is both easy and dangerous to generalise. *Everything depends on the actual situation."*

In support of these arguments many illustrations could be culled from the Western Front and other theatres during the late war. One of the lessons of the Battle of Neuve Chapelle was the efficacy of the bombing of enemy railway communications. Again, in the Battle of Loos, one of the main functions of our aircraft was to prevent the arrival of reinforcements and ammunition on the enemy front attack, by means of bombing attacks, and an attempt to block the railway between the junction two miles north of Valenciennes inclusive and Douai exclusive.

Referring to these latter operations, the Commander-in-Chief, in his despatch, writes: " Aircraft performed valuable work by undertaking distant flights behind the enemy's lines, and by successfully blowing up railways, wrecking trains, and damaging stations on his lines of communications by means of bomb attacks." There were, in addition, instances of ammunition dumps and trains being blown up as a result of air attack, which had the effect of either postponing a contemplated operation or seriously affecting operations in progress through a shortage of ammunition caused thereby.

From the foregoing arguments the following guiding rules can be deduced:—

Firstly, that in static warfare or when two armies have come to battle, air attacks (tactical) should be pursued relentlessly on the enemy's lines of communications immediately behind the battle front of the troops engaged; in point of fact, attacks should be made on those targets that will directly assist in the battle itself, *i.e.*, on those points which are of immediate vital concern and of tactical importance to the enemy.

Secondly, that during the period before the opposing armies have joined battle, *i.e.*, during concentration and the advance from the area of concentration, air attacks (strategical) should be concentrated on those points of strategical importance to the enemy.

Thirdly, that during a war of movement both strategical and tactical air attacks will probably be made, concentration being carried out on either the tactical or strategical points that are of immediate vital importance. These points will depend on the situation and circumstances of the moment.

During all such operations, it will be the primary duty of fighting aircraft to carry out a sustained air offensive against the enemy's air forces, in order to give freedom of movement to bombers and other aircraft and to prevent the enemy from gaining any benefit from his own.

It can with all truth be asserted that it was realized early by the belligerents (at least, on the Western Front) that final victory in the war would in all probability be gained by that side possessing a marked air superiority, and " that whichever side allowed itself to be outbidden in that conquest, forfeited its powers of probing the dispositions and plans of the other, and relinquished the power of striking at long-range as well as losing to the army one of its most powerful weapons of offence and defence. Tanks, cavalry, artillery and infantry would have been deprived of a freedom to act analogous to that which sea power affords an army."

In conclusion, we may again point to one of the basic principles of all warfare, mobility. The army of the future must be organized in such a manner that its mobility is increased. The period both of concentration and of the advance from the concentration area must be cut down to a minimum. The longer time the armies require for these processes, the greater will be the risk (and a serious one) from air attacks. The more an army is dependent upon fixed and limited lines of communications, the more vulnerable it becomes, hence the need for increased mobility.

The methods of employing aircraft in co-operation with an army may be summarized as follows :—

Firstly, the employment of the fighting squadrons from the commencement of the campaign in offensive action against the enemy's air forces. Their duty will be to gain air superiority within that area over which it is intended the operations on the ground will take place. To ensure success, concentration of effort is essential.

Secondly, it will be their duty, if the air situation admits, to support the attacks of our own Army by direct attacks on the enemy's troops. Their primary object must, however, always be kept in view—that of gaining and maintaining air superiority—and decisions to employ them in subsidiary rôles must be taken only in exceptional and extreme cases.

It is interesting to study the instructions contained in the German post-war Training Regulations on this subject, notes on which appeared in *The Army Quarterly* of July, 1924. Although the actual organization of the squadrons and their allotment of duties may be matters of controversy, yet, so far as the actual employment of these forces is concerned, there can be little doubt as to its efficiency. In point of fact, they are but a reiteration of the methods proved and adopted by our own air forces during the war, lessons which the Germans have not been slow to learn.

German aircraft are divided into observation units and fighting units, the latter being sub-divided into battle squadrons, bombing squadrons and pursuit squadrons. It is to the employment of these three types in particular that attention must be directed.

The employment of strong fighting formations at the outset of a campaign is foreshadowed with the object of influencing the opponent's measures during the period of strategic deployment, and the necessity is indicated of concentrating a superiority of fighting units over the decisive points of the ground operations. It is even stated that formations not taking part in the *decisive* fight must at this time dispense with aircraft.

As regards the employment of battle squadrons, the instructions are as follows :—

In the attack.—It is laid down that when the enemy

is occupying easily recognizable features, aircraft should be sent in simultaneously with the infantry assault, against the point where it is important that the enemy's resistance should be broken quickly.

In the defence.—When the preparatory positions of the enemy's infantry can be located, a determined attack by battle squadrons kept in hand for this purpose may break the weight of the hostile attack or delay it; their objectives will, however, usually be farther back—hostile reserves, groups of batteries, reinforcements, etc.

Bombing Squadrons.—The employment of these squadrons would not seem to differ materially from the strategical and tactical considerations that have been advanced in this chapter.

Pursuit Squadrons.—The special mission of these squadrons is laid down as "to obtain mastery of the air" (air superiority). With this object, hostile aircraft are to be sought out *behind* the enemy's lines and brought to battle, and so forced on the defensive. These squadrons are also called on to support and protect reconnaissance squadrons, and in this connection it may be remarked that this should be effectively accomplished by the former action.

During battle the enemy's observation aircraft are cited as the principal objectives of attack by these squadrons, whilst the protection of their own infantry and artillery against hostile aircraft comes within their scope.

In defence the bulk of the pursuit squadrons are to be kept back until the beginning of the infantry attack, when they are to be launched against the probable mass attack of hostile aircraft.

On this last paragraph there may be divergence of opinion. The chief argument against it, and a strong one, lies in the fact that the air offensive must be both vigorous and sustained, and air activity is not confined to the period of a ground attack, but, more often than not—as was freely demonstrated during the war—it was a prelude to the offensive operations undertaken by the army. The policy, therefore, of keeping such squadrons in hand is not a wise one, and the whole of the air forces should be employed at all times to carry out a relentless pressure on the enemy's aircraft. If this is done, air superiority—an essential prelude to successful operations—will be gained and so give that freedom of action which is so necessary. The division of duties of the battle and pursuit squadrons is of doubtful utility at the present stage of development, but may in course of time prove of value.

The instructions quoted follow closely the experiences gained during the war, as the following extract from a despatch from the Commander-in-Chief of the British Armies in France will clearly illustrate:—

" During the past year the part played by the Royal Flying Corps in modern battles has grown more and more important. Each successive attack has served to demonstrate with increasing clearness the paramount necessity for the closest co-operation between air and land arms. All must work together on a general plan towards our end—the defeat of the enemy forces.

" Air fighting has taken place on an ever-increasing scale in order to enable the machines engaged upon these tasks to carry out their work.

" A definite air offensive, in which long distance raiding has taken a prominent part, has become a recognised part of the preparations for infantry attack.

" Throughout the progress of the battle itself, low-flying aeroplanes not only maintain contact with our advancing infantry, reporting their positions and signalling the earliest indications of hostile counter-attack, but themselves join directly in the attack by engaging the enemy's infantry in line and in support with both machine gun fire and bombs, by assisting our artillery to disperse hostile concentrations, and by spreading confusion among the enemy's transport, reinforcements and batteries.

" In answer to the concentrations of hostile machines on our Front and the strenuous efforts made by the

H

enemy to reassert himself in the air, the bombing of German aerodromes has been intensified and has been carried out at great distance behind the enemy's lines. In more than one instance the enemy has been compelled to abandon particular aerodromes altogether as the result of our constant raids.

"The enemy's railway stations and communications, his dumps and billets have been attacked with *increasing frequency* and with most successful results."

The many functions of air forces in battle are thus set clearly before us and fully demonstrate the value and effect which this new arm has on land battles of to-day.

One further point to which reference must here be made is the vulnerability of transport ships to aircraft attack. The peculiar characteristic of an army embarked for distant operations is its helplessness whilst afloat. It is paralysed for effective action during the period of transit. An enemy who holds flanking positions upon the lines of communication, especially in narrow waters, will be a constant source of danger to movements by sea. Whether a convoy can put to sea before superiority in the air has been decided may be disputed, but this must depend upon actual conditions prevailing, such as the distance of the route to be taken by the convoy and the position of the ports of embarkation in relation to the enemy's aircraft bases.

It will be the duty of the Air Force to secure the communications as a preliminary to this concentration. The situation must be such that the dispatch of any expedition overseas can be carried out without serious molestation from enemy aircraft.

It will be the duty of the Air Force in connection with overseas transport of troops to safeguard them in transit from enemy air attack, and to co-operate with the Navy in securing sea communications.

During disembarkation and concentration it will be the duty of the Air Force to prevent any enemy aircraft from attacking the point of disembarkation, to prevent his obtaining information, and to attack his lines of communication and strategical points, depots and concentration centres, in order to delay his action.

The selection of the base or bases of an army and the concentration area will have to be made with a view to security from aircraft attack, or conversely our own aircraft must be able to defend these bases effectively against enemy air attack.

The employment of air forces during the advance or retreat of an army presents many interesting possibilities. The enormous increase of modern armies, the power of modern weapons, and the many new factors that increase the difficulties of movement of these modern armies, have limited the chances of surprise and made the lines of communication more vulnerable.

Whether aircraft will be of more value in an advance or retreat must depend upon circumstances and, incidentally, on the degree of air superiority possessed. Again, where the lines of retreat or advance are restricted by geographical conditions, the vulnerability of those lines will increase with the limitations imposed. A classic instance of this occurred in Palestine in 1918. The enemy's retreat was cut off to the north and only one line of retirement was left open to the Turkish columns, across the River Jordan, with the result that the enemy's guns, transport and troops were so congested that they could not escape from the devastating attacks of our aircraft, and surrendered to the British Army.

General Maurice writes:* " Pursuit after battle is one of the most difficult operations of war and the number of successful pursuits even by highly trained armies is small. It is possible that pursuit in the air may be a normal sequel of future victories, and have results as deadly as those of Allenby's air pursuit in the battles of Megiddo, but as the nervous strain of battle increases pursuit on land is likely to be less than more frequent."

The primary object of all air operations in a retreat must be to endeavour to turn retreat into a rout by a con-

Governments and War.

tinual offensive against the retreating enemy columns. The degree of success will be dependent on the degree of air superiority. If the latter is such that we are able to concentrate the whole of our air strength against the retreating columns with little interference from the enemy's air forces, success will be assured. The nature of the country and the lines of communication over which the enemy's retreat lies, will also determine to a very large extent the opportunities afforded our aircraft in attacking successfully the enemy's army.

In a pursuit, aircraft will be employed to harass continuously, by all the means in its power, the enemy's rear organization and lines of communication. Every effort must be made to hamper his retreat, by blocking his communications, by means of attacks on important rail and road junctions and on large centres of activity. They are of particular value in the pursuit of a beaten army and may turn a retreat into a rout. A few illustrations of this will suffice.

" Throughout the day the roads, packed with the enemy's troops and transport, afforded excellent targets to our airmen, who took full advantage of their opportunities despite the unfavourable weather. Over thirty guns, which bombs and machine gun fire from the air had forced the enemy to abandon, were captured by a battalion of the 25th Division in the fields near Le Priseau."—Commander-in-Chief, British Armies in France. Despatch dated December 21st, 1918.

" The superiority established by the Air Force over the enemy was one of the great factors in the success of my troops.

" Great confusion reigned at Tul Keram. Bodies of troops, guns, motor lorries and transport of every description were endeavouring to escape along the road leading to Messudieh and Nablus. This road, which follows the railway up a narrow valley, was already crowded with troops and transport. The confusion was added to by the persistent attacks of the Royal Air Force and Australian Flying Corps, from which there was no escape. Great havoc was caused, and in several places the road was blocked by overturned lorries and vehicles. . . .

"Considerable confusion existed behind the enemy's rearguards. All day his transport had been withdrawing. The Messudieh-Jenin Road was crowded. Its defiles had been bombed continuously by the Royal Air Force, as had long columns of troops and transport moving on Nablus in order to reach the Besian Road. . . ."—Despatch dated June 28th, 1919.

"The R.A.F. took a very prominent part in the battle, harassing the enemy's retreat so effectually that many batteries and thousands of prisoners fell into our hands that would have otherwise escaped."—Extract from despatch of G.O.C.-in-C., British Forces in Italy, dated November 15th, 1918.

"The R.F.C. by bombing and machine gun fire caused many casualties and much confusion amongst the retreating columns of the enemy and their transport."—General C.-in.C., Mesopotamia, April, 15th, 1918.

"The head of the transport column was heavily bombed. The drivers left their vehicles in panic, wagons overturned and in a short time the road was completely blocked.

"A column, with transport and guns, ten miles long, was attacked by the R.A.F. The column broke up and abandoned its guns and transport.

"On the 24th April, 1916, our aeroplanes made a bomb and machine gun attack from a low altitude on the enemy's troops left in Qatia, causing very heavy casualties and destroying the camp. On the morning of the 25th, further attacks were made by our aircraft on enemy forces at Bir el Abd and Bir el Bayud. These attacks were extremely successful, working great havoc among men and animals. . . . Chiefly through the efforts of our pilots the enemy was made to pay a very heavy price for his partially successful raid."—Operations in Palestine, October 31st, 1918.

With regard to the operations indicated here, the character of the country must be fully borne in mind. There was little in the way of cover. The lines of communications were very restricted, causing a congestion of traffic. This afforded aircraft an easy task in picking out the enemy's columns and in attacking them.

AIRCRAFT IN THE DEFENCE.

The duties of the air force attached to an army on the defensive will be to locate the hostile columns, to report on their disposition and movements both before and during the battle, to assist the defending artillery by locating targets and observing fire, to furnish information regarding any changes in the dispositions of friendly troops by means of contact patrols, to give notice of hostile reinforcements, to destroy communications beyond artillery range by bombs, and to inflict casualties on reserves and reinforcements by dropping bombs and by machine gun fire. The execution of these duties presupposes an *offensive* attitude, so as to maintain local air superiority.

" During a retirement the air forces must be particularly active in endeavouring to prevent the enemy's aircraft from harassing the retiring troops, and also in low-flying action against his advanced troops.

" Used in large numbers they may delay a pursuit and thereby give a retiring force time to disengage and reform. The moral effect of these means of attack is great and not confined to the material damage inflicted."
—Field Service Regulations, 1920.

General von Hoeppner, who commanded the German Air Service during the last two years of the war, alludes to the ceaseless offensive kept up by the French Air Service at Verdun. Attacks by low-flying aircraft, he says, so hit the moral of the German infantry that a cry went up for an " air barrage," and it is important to note that a policy of defence was adopted.

It is interesting at this point to recapitulate the instructions contained in our own Field Service Regulations dealing with aircraft in the attack and defence.

The duties of the air force in the attack are two-fold: offensive action and reconnaissance. " The essential preliminary to all other air work is to gain at least a local and temporary superiority in the air. Unless this is done, not only are the machines prevented from accomplishing their other duties, but the enemy's machines are able to co-operate with his infantry and artillery and to harass the attacking troops without interference. The chief means of obtaining superiority is by a bold use of the *offensive* designed to drive back hostile machines and *force them to fight at a distance* behind their own lines.

" 1. Once air superiority has been established offensive action against the enemy's troops and transport by means of machine gun fire and bombs, by low-flying machines under the protection of high patrols, becomes feasible, and must be vigorously undertaken. Whenever possible machines must be specially detailed to deal with anti-tank guns, and when the enemy has not had time to dig his guns in, special efforts must be made to harass battery and wagon lines.

" 2. Attacks by low-flying aeroplanes, however, are expensive in casualties to machines and personnel. They should be restricted, therefore, to occasions when really favourable targets are presented, *e.g.*, during the few hours following a surprise attack when there is sure to be confusion behind the enemy's lines. Every effort must be made to keep the Air Force constantly informed as to the progress of the battle.

" 3. Offensive action against the enemy's communications must be carried out by bomb raids, but it is usually best to defer such action until a few hours after the assault has been launched, *i.e.*, until such time as activity on his communications is likely to begin.

" 4. During the hours of darkness every effort must be made to disturb the enemy's rest and interfere with movements behind his lines by means of continuous bombing raids.

"The moral effect of such raids, apart from the material effects of interference with the enemy's food and ammunition supplies, is very great and tends to lower the moral of his fighting troops. To prevent the enemy harassing our own troops in the same manner it is essential that A.A. guns and searchlights be pushed forward, as the attack progresses, close behind the leading troops, so that they may be in a position to engage the enemy's night bombing machines before they reach our lines, and that the anti-aircraft defences of billeting areas of reserves and resting troops should be organized in detail."

The value of aircraft on the flank of a retreating or an advancing army must also depend on similar circumstances, and it would be interesting here to discover how and to what extent the opening movements of the late war might have been affected in the first few weeks on the Western Front if air forces had reached their present-day development.

There is, I think, no doubt, that the whole of the German air forces employed on the Western Front would have been thrown into the scale in the active support of their land campaign. For this reason, if for no other, it can scarcely be disputed that Germany could not have contemplated aircraft attacks on England at least during the first few weeks or months of the operations of her armies which were vital to her. Circumstances, therefore, might have dictated the expediency of attacking the ports of disembarkation of the British Army. If a sufficient force had thus been available for these operations and they could have attained a marked superiority in the air in the area of those ports, no British force could have been landed and we should thus have been forced to abandon any hope of employing our military forces on the enemy's right flank and compelled to seek more secure bases further south. The result would have been that our military forces could not have reached the theatre of their operations in time to render effective aid.

General von Staabs, of the German General Staff, has drawn a lurid picture of the chaos that would have been brought into the German mobilization plan in August, 1914, had any failure occurred on the railways used by the right wing of the German armies between Cologne and Aix-la-Chapelle. Had aircraft been more developed at the time, this fact also must not be overlooked, that, in the war under discussion, Germany would have been in a relatively weak position, geographically, with regard to the air. She would have been open to instant attack from the air forces of three great powers—France, Great Britain and Russia. Although we can presume that Austria would have undoubtedly neutralized the strength of Russia in this respect, the air strength of Germany alone might reasonably have been insufficient to ensure her successful attainment of air superiority over the combined forces of France and Great Britain. And I think that we can here draw a useful corollary in regard to the air. Whereas few nations possess a fleet, all nations will possess air forces, the strength of which may not necessarily be determined on the same relative principles as those which have determined the strength of navies.

These facts are plain from a most cursory study of the subject. The point, therefore, which I wish to make clear is that the combination of the air forces of any two belligerents might conceivably be far stronger relatively than the combinations of fleets with which we have been so accustomed to reckon in the past.

It must also be remembered that, given the manufacturing facilities, air forces are created far more easily and rapidly than navies. The facilities for rapid expansion are a matter of extreme importance, and emphasize the very important part which a flourishing civil aviation must take in any scheme of expansion of air forces in time of war. The nation that possesses these will have the necessary organization, which it will be able to turn to good account immediately on the outbreak of war.

The increasing importance of operations in the air will affect the plans of the other services both in regard to the security of their own air bases and to the possibility of the occupation of territory within which enemy air bases are established, which directly threaten the security of any military forces. The effective employment of air forces may depend on the success attending the naval or military operations which may be directed against the enemy's aircraft bases.

To revert to the late war, air forces might reasonably have changed the whole conception of the German strategic plan on the Western Front in 1914. These plans are too well known to need repetition. The question that automatically occurs to our minds from the facts already narrated is, "Could the enveloping movement through Belgium have succeeded and would it have been a practicable proposition?" We will presume that a powerful French air concentration had been effected in the region of Alsace and Lorraine. This force would have held a commanding position in which to act on the flank and in rear of the German armies and have been ideally situated for attacking the German lines of communication and concentration centres. In addition, the whole of the bridgeheads over the Rhine, the important strategic railway centres, would have been menaced from the air. Not only this. The most important factories and industrial centres situated along the Rhine Valley would have been open to attack from the French squadrons. The problem thus presented to the German High Command would in those circumstances, therefore, have been a very different one. The area in which this French air concentration was situated would have become an objective for primary consideration, and it is reasonable to presume that the German strategic plan would have been based on occupying this area and thus depriving the French of such an important position.

The conclusion, then, at which we must arrive is that the war on this front might very well have undergone a complete change. To carry the argument still further, we might assume French air power to have been sufficiently strong to combat the German air forces and to have gained air superiority within the first week or fortnight. The effect of this would have been that the military defence of France would have been materially assisted and that much valuable time would have been accorded her for holding the German attack. Any delay which must inevitably have resulted would have increased the risk of failure of the German land campaign, from the fact that armies and lines of communication would have been subjected for a greater period to the attack of the French air squadrons.

There are many other interesting and practical assumptions which can be made in analysing the effect which air power is now capable of asserting on such operations as I have described. We need go no further here into these problems; but it may be mentioned that the strategical advantage of attack from the air would have been entirely with the French.

Then in regard to the Eastern Front we see that Russia would have possessed the strategical advantage over both Austria and Germany. The more important centres in both these countries would have been open to an attack from the Russian air forces, which could have been situated within but a short distance of those centres. Again, Russia, by virtue of her enormous tracts of country and vastly dispersed strategic centres of importance, would have presented a relatively more difficult problem to her enemies, and air attack by either Austria or Germany could not have attained the same degree of success. Armies passing over the Carpathians would have presented vulnerable targets for aircraft attack.

The geographical features of countries will play an important part in the strategy of air warfare as they do in that on sea or land.

The vulnerability of armies to air attack is chiefly due to the fact that their strategical movement is governed by fixed lines of communication. The ability possessed by aircraft to attack armies, their depots, railheads, ammunition dumps, etc., will necessitate a radical change in the constitution of armies and the means of forcing a strategical or tactical decision on land. In this connection we must not neglect to take into consideration present and future developments of land armaments, more especially those increasing the mobility and offensive power of an army.

In conclusion, the following extract from an article on Anti-Aircraft Defence* may be quoted as being in all respects a common-sense summary of the problem. "The 'Achilles heel' of the modern Army, from the air point of view, is the long lines of transport with, so to speak, its one-dimensional movement. Now that hostile action is not confined to the immediate battle-front [a point which is so often forgotten by many, not realized by some, and ignored by others who do not wish to profit by victory], every effort must be made to avoid offering massed targets to the air. Cross-country traction will undoubtedly relieve us of many of our difficulties in this respect. For some time to come, however, we are faced with the slow moving lines of traffic, part of it with a terribly vulnerable means of traction, namely, the horse. As much forethought should be given to defeating the air menace by protective disposition as is given to covering the flanks of the battle line. So long as traffic has to keep to roads, and so long as rivers have to be crossed by bridges, there are bound to be cases where the bunching of traffic is inevitable. Let these cases be kept down to a minimum, and then active A.A. defence will be able to cope with the situation to a great extent. . . . If we give the aeroplane a favourable target, such as troops or vehicles massed together, the results may be very considerable if not disastrous. . . . The moral lies in the folly of offering a target of such a nature."

**The Army Quarterly*, April, 1924. Capt. K. M. Loch.

Finally, what is likely to be the effect on land warfare generally as the direct result of this new power of air attack? There will be a gradual evolution towards the increase of the mobility of troops, guns and transport, and less reliance will be placed on roads and railways or fixed communications. We can picture the armies of the future breaking away from the traditional means of movement and being transported across country. This accelerated mobility will ensure greater manœuvrability, and this, coupled with the powers of attack possessed by a superior air arm, may once again give armies that power of carrying out an enveloping movement and thus inflicting a crushing defeat.

AIR TRANSPORT OF TROOPS.

I need only touch on this feature in order to show its possibilities in the future. That air transport is feasible has already been demonstrated and it is capable of reaching still greater dimensions. There will be many and varied opportunities for its use in future warfare, and perhaps one illustration may suffice to prove the important strategical and tactical results which may be expected from it. The opportunities presented will, no doubt, be dependent in great measure on the geographical features of the country in which a war is being waged, and in such countries as Iraq, the Middle East, and where the fronts of armies cannot be continuous (which was possible in the late war in Europe), it will be possible to transport a few hundred men with ammunition and machine guns, etc., to the flank or rear of an enemy army. Such an operation, if conducted at the right time and place as a surprise, is capable of achieving great strategical or tactical results. One has only to study the operations conducted during the late war in Palestine and Mesopotamia to see the ample opportunities afforded for this type of operation and the results such an operation might have achieved during certain periods. The very fact that such operations are possible in any future war will not be without its effect upon the disposition of armies.

CHAPTER VII.

CONCLUSIONS.

"If we are to profit by the experience of war, let our thoughts travel on lines that lead to useful conclusions."—Earl Grey.

To our Empire more than to any other nation, air power is indispensable. It is incumbent upon every citizen to appreciate to the full the potentialities of aircraft as an instrument of war. None can foresee what the future development of engineering holds in store. It has not, however, been my intention to plunge into the future or to advance arguments based on pure speculation. It is good to possess foresight, which is quite another matter. It will suffice if we remind those who have powers of prognostication that wars cannot be waged on speculation. In many respects, my work may be found incomplete. That is inevitable. My subject cannot be dealt with fully within the compass of one small volume. I have accordingly sought to confine myself to the more important issues, avoiding unnecessary detail as far as possible.

In this book, every endeavour has been made, from a study of operations during the late war, to deduce certain conclusions which appear to be of permanent application to the employment of air forces. It is, perhaps, not surprising that there should be the same fundamental principles in the employment of air forces as in the employment of a navy or an army. Much value is to be derived from the strategy of both, more especially, perhaps, from that of the Navy, which is, indeed, natural, seeing that the sea possesses a closer analogy in its two-dimensional movement.

I have not attempted to deal with the tactical employment of aircraft. My main purpose has been to explore the functions of the new arm in all the broader aspects of warfare, to arrive at a common air doctrine, and to define what, in my opinion, are sound principles of air warfare. Doubtless these principles will change but little; it is only in their application that the further development of this arm will affect them.

Air warfare is a subject on which much has been written, but no one, I think, has attempted to do more than outline the many functions of aircraft. By the majority of writers, too much stress has been laid on the horrors that this form of warfare is capable of inflicting on the civilian population. This has led to the conclusion that it will be possible for future wars to be brought to an end by aircraft acting alone. There are other writers who, with an exaggerated estimate of the offensive capabilities of this arm, have treated the subject wholly from the offensive aspect, ignoring both the limitations of aircraft and the counter-measures of defence. It is as well to realize that, while air forces can conduct certain operations without the aid of sea or land forces, the relative value of these two arms remains, and that *great* wars of the future will only be concluded successfully *by the combined action of all three*.

The purpose of this book is not to "create" principles, but rather, by a study of facts, to interpret the principles that exist.

The following is a quotation from an article written by Air Chief Marshal Sir Hugh Trenchard, which appeared in *The Army Quarterly* of April, 1921:—

"When we come to consider the employment of the Royal Air Force, the first want we feel is that there is but little literature on the subject. . . . It must not be thought that there are no principles of tactics or strategy for the air. The principles are there. Principles are not opinions, but facts, and are unchangeable through all the changing types of machines of war. But what is the trouble? It is that these principles have not been formulated by a Hamley or Mahan, and that they have not been accepted by the outside world. But the principles formed in the last years of the war were formed in the same way as they were formed in the past. They were not created; facts made them, and they exist and are sound. But at the same time the coming of the air service means that the application of old principles of warfare must be carefully studied to see in what way the application of the principles should be modified. Time and space problems in aviation differ entirely from those which confront the naval and military commander. The moral factor is enormously enhanced in comparison with the material. There are no physical obstacles. We have, however, the experience of war in many theatres to guide us, although it has not yet been committed to paper in any readily accessible form. . . . In my opinion the most important principle of all, and the one perhaps least generally understood and appreciated, is that the work of the air service either on land or sea, in spite of its many and various aspects, can only achieve its greatest efficiency if regarded and carried out as a single co-ordinated effort. The work required, whether by the Navy or Army, is both tactical and strategical. It consists of reconnaissance and photography, spotting for artillery, and of offensive action against troops or ships, against personnel and *matériel* on lines of communications, depots and harbours. Independently of this work *in intimate co-operation with the other Services* the Air Force can attack the enemy's sources of supply and the moral of his civil population and government."

With regard to this latter point, it is interesting to note the Air Chief Marshal later emphasizes the important fact that "All bombing, even when carried out on very distant and apparently independent objectives, *must be co-ordinated with the efforts that are being made by the land and sea forces,* both as to the selection of objectives and as to the time at which the attacks shall take place." He further emphasizes the important fact that, whatever the nature of the air work undertaken, whether it be in conjunction with sea or land forces, or independent of either, "*it is utterly wrong and wasteful to look upon them as entirely separate duties. In the first place, to perform any of them with success it is necessary to gain superiority in the air.*"

With regard to "Surprise," he mentions that this principle "is as important in the air as on the ground, though harder to obtain. For one thing, the need for exerting constant pressure conflicts with surprise, but, at the same time, surprise can be used with great effect in the air, owing to the power of being able to switch off from one point of attack on to another, very often with hardly any movement of aerodromes."

A study of all these principles has been made at some length, and it is hoped that sound conclusions have been drawn therefrom.

It must always be remembered that whenever a new weapon has been evolved, counter-measures are immediately put in hand by which to restrict, as much as possible, its offensive powers. This new weapon, more correctly termed "arm," presents, by its very nature, a problem in many respects different from any other hitherto produced. Its limitations in some respects are fewer and its powers to some extent are greater. Whether its powers outweigh its limitations is a debatable point. If we neglect to consider counter-measures, we shall be liable to over-rate its powers of offence, with results that may lead not only to disappointment, but possibly disaster. On the other hand, we must constantly weigh up in our minds the merits and demerits of each and every particular form of offensive and defensive device that is evolved, for unless we do so we can never hope to employ the forces at our disposal effectively or economically.

The main conclusion to be drawn from the foregoing chapters is that aircraft are absolutely indispensable to the success of any operation of war in the future, whether by sea or land, though they will never usurp the functions of either fleets or armies in the general strategic plan, but will be the essential complement to the functions of these arms.

The necessity for the control of certain air units by the Fleet and Army for specialized work in connection with these services has been shown to be vital if they may rely on a strong and efficient air arm to enable them to carry out their functions effectively. Success in war can only be attained by a whole-hearted co-operation between all three services and this is only made possible if complete understanding exists and vested interests are cast aside. The reverses of one service cannot be dissociated from the reverses of another, and success can only be assured by a common strategy and a common concentration of effort in its execution.

It may safely be said that aircraft will be a strategical factor of great value in all naval, military and combined operations. It may be laid down as an axiom that the first step towards winning the war is to establish air superiority in the area over which operations are to be undertaken, and that the extent to which bombing operations will be conducted will depend relatively upon the initial success against the opposing air forces. The power to attack must depend upon certain conditions, chief among which will be the relative strengths of the belligerents and the geographical situation of air bases. The less risk of attack on our bombers, the greater will be the success of their operations, as it will enable them to extend their attacks further afield than would otherwise be the case.

I am of the opinion that against *civilized* nations air attack of itself will not be conclusive, unless the power of attack far outstrips that now available.

Operations against semi-civilized and uncivilized states since the war have proved that air power is able, with little or no assistance from either the Army or

Navy, to attain complete success in bringing hostile tribes to submission.

For the sake of clarity, the chief strategic powers of aircraft are summarized under two headings:—

(a) Operations influencing sea warfare.
(b) Operations influencing land warfare.

(a) *Operations influencing Sea Warfare.*

Aircraft will be able—

(1) To attack merchant shipping and thereby increase the difficulty of maintaining control of the sea communications.

(2) To attack the enemy's commercial ports, and thus hinder the movement of ships, and the importation of food or munitions and merchandise, thus increasing the effectiveness of economic blockade.

(3) To attack ships of all classes and to force a fleet from the shelter of its ports and harbours into others of less strategic value.

(4) To attack the docks, workshops, etc., of vital importance to the navy.

(5) To give a commander greater liberty of action, by their power of covering the movements of his own forces and of obtaining information of those of the enemy. They will, in addition, place in his hands a quicker means of gaining contact, and will facilitate reconnaissance generally. They will also expedite communication generally between his forces, and be a means of maintaining contact with the forces of the enemy whose movements should be accurately and speedily reported throughout a battle.

(b) *Operations influencing Land Warfare.*

(1) Aircraft will be able to extend the area of operations far behind the enemy's lines, and to carry the war into the enemy's country.

(2) By attacking an enemy's communications and supplies, they will add to the difficulty of maintaining them.

(3) By continuous attacks on troops in reserve or at rest, they will have the effect of greatly diminishing their fighting value.

(4) They provide an ideal weapon for pursuit of a defeated enemy.

(5) They facilitate retreat.

(6) They expedite the gaining of information concerning the movements of the enemy.

(7) In support of land forces they place in the hands of a commander an additional weapon of great tactical importance and power of attack.

A strategic air offensive will be more and more effective as the range and power of aircraft increase, and as the precision with which they are able to operate is developed. It must again be emphasized that none of the operations outlined above can be successfully accomplished without first gaining "air superiority." I may have laboured this point, but I regard its importance worthy of repetition.

Col. Fuller, in his naval prize essay which appeared in the *R.U.S.I. Journal* for 1920, in the section dealing with the future development of aircraft, writes: "Aircraft in war have been proved to be useful for four main purposes: bombing, scouting, ranging and offensive action against craft of their own nature. It has been stated that 'the rôle of the aeroplane is essentially offensive'; this, however, is only correct when applied to a contest between aeroplanes, for the experiences of the war go to prove that the aeroplane has little offensive power against *armoured* troops on land and still less against armoured ships at sea. Not a single British warship was destroyed by aircraft, neither was the British Merchant Service seriously annoyed by them."

Most of the points raised herein have been treated at great length in this book, and I propose here to deal with them only in a very direct way. The experiences of the war proved beyond any doubt that the offensive power of aircraft was of very great importance. Col. Fuller is perhaps correct in confining his argument to one against *armoured* troops and ships at sea. Their offensive rôle is not confined to either. The important fact is that aircraft can attack strategic positions denied to armies and navies. In the case of armies, they can attack strategic positions and vital points in lines of communication, concentration centres, and so on; with regard to sea warfare, the naval bases and dockyards. Furthermore, they are able to attack the means of production on which both armies and navies alike depend for their supplies. With regard to the statement that no British warship was destroyed and that the Merchant Service was not seriously annoyed by aircraft, it is a sufficient rejoinder that no serious attacks were ever attempted, chiefly because they were for the most part out of range of the aircraft that had so far been developed.

It is essential, when we are considering the influence that air forces will have in the conduct of war, that we should bear in mind the difference between a continental country and an island.

Some considerable time must elapse before the population of a continental country will feel the loss of external communications seriously, and the time taken to produce the desired effect is relative to the size of the country, its geographical situation, and the extent of its dependence on external communications.

Whereas in the past sea warfare was the only method by which interference with the economic life of a country was possible, in the future a combination of sea and air attack will be far more effective.

On the other hand, any interference with the external communications of an island causes far more distress among the population, owing to its dependence on sea communications. The success of the air arm, however, will be dependent upon the opportunities offered by its geographical position in relation to the hostile country.

The strength or size of an air force must depend on many considerations, the more important of which are the following :—

(1) The vulnerability of the country to be defended.
(2) The commitments necessary for the defence of overseas possessions.
(3) The protection of sea communications.
(4) The efficiency and strength of the air forces of prospective enemies.
(5) The force that it is estimated will be required to carry out strategic operations.
(6) The force necessary to ensure the success of sea and land operations.

No hard and fast rule as to a power standard can be laid down. Numbers alone cannot determine the issue. A high standard of fighting efficiency both in personnel, armament and equipment, a steady source of reserves, and a sound organization based on war requirements are the most important attributes of any service, and these must be our first consideration in expending the money granted by the State to the air service.

Apart from the considerations outlined, it must be borne in mind that both our sea and land forces are useless as protective services against air attack. Our Air Force is alone capable of dealing with the enemy's air forces, and if this force is not capable of gaining superiority in the air then our sea and land forces of themselves will be unable to save the situation. Again, neither our sea nor our land forces will be able to carry out their respective functions effectively in the absence of an air force that can ensure the defeat of the enemy's air forces.

As shown in Chapter II, our striking force must be ready for immediate action on the outbreak of hostilities and our entire air service of sufficient strength to gain and maintain air superiority. Behind this force our organization must be such as to ensure that our losses may be made good immediately, and this can only be done by husbanding and organizing our resources in skilled personnel, *matériel*, training and production in peace time. In this respect, we must rely principally on a flourishing civil aviation, on the formation of squadrons on a territorial basis, and on the promotion of civilian flying clubs.

But here a word of warning. In the event of a European war in which we become involved, it will be impossible to meet the many demands which will inevitably arise throughout the Empire. The possession of an empire, with its many local and widely-separated problems of defence, has always caused the diversion of unnecessarily large forces. Future demands for aircraft are likely to be as large if not larger than those to which we have been accustomed in the past, so far as naval or military forces are concerned. The dispatch of air units to these fronts from the main theatre will be fraught with grave consequences. "The British Empire was won in battles on and around the continent of Europe, and not by means of local successes in distant theatres overseas; and it was victory in the continental theatre and nothing else which in the past enabled these local successes to bear fruit."*

Our available forces must therefore be so disposed that we can obtain decisive results in the main theatre of war.

Additional commitments outside the main theatre would be a serious drain on our resources. The inevitable conclusion is that these future demands must of necessity be met from other sources within the Empire— Canada, Australia, New Zealand, India and South Africa. We may hope that the development of the air forces within those countries will be commensurate with the Empire's safety. In this connection, it is true to say that, whereas our Dominions have hitherto relied on the Mother Country for their protection, owing to our possession of a fleet second to none, no such complete reliance can be placed on this country for the same provision in the air.

Nor is it expected, as is proved by the fact that this question was fully explored at the last Imperial Conference, when the following resolution was recorded:—

*Direction of War. Bird.

"The desirability of the development of the Air Forces in the several countries of the Empire upon such lines as will make it possible, by means of the adoption, as far as practicable, of a common system of organization and training and the use of uniform manuals, patterns of arms, equipment and stores (with the exception of the type of aircraft) for each part of the Empire as it may determine *to co-operate with other parts with the least possible delay and the greatest efficiency.*"

I have put into *italics* the most important part of this resolution, and if the whole of it is faithfully observed, we need have little fear as to the future.

Nevertheless, the most critical portion of our Empire communications is left untouched by the scheme, and remains to be secured. I allude to our communications through the Mediterranean to the East, Egypt, Iraq and India. It appears that the defence throughout these areas will have to be provided by the Mother Country, and in view of its intrinsic importance, it seems likely to make an increasingly heavy demand upon our resources. For some years we may not be threatened with another war in Europe, but this state of affairs will not last indefinitely. We must be prepared for any eventuality. The time is not far distant when our air forces will be moved from one locality to another in accordance with the ever-changing political situation. This course is analogous to that of our fleet, which, as we know, was concentrated in home waters prior to 1914 to meet the German menace. That menace removed, the fleet is concentrated in other waters where our security can be most vitally threatened. Air forces are comparable to naval forces; provided they have their bases within effective distance of each other they need not be localized. A system of such bases throughout the Empire's long lines of communications renders defence more mobile and lessens the need for tying up units in a number of places for local defence.

" Assuming there must always be places in which

there were fixed defences, there was every advantage to be gained by making our Empire defences as *mobile* as ever they could, and of being able to transfer them as quickly as they could from one part to another. That had been the policy of the Government. Its great strength was its *mobility*. That was the very basis of Empire air policy—not that they should scatter a few aeroplanes in a large number of places, but have their concentration of aeroplanes in this and that centre, and their air bases organized between them."*

" When the Dominions and the Empire are linked with the Mother Country, and, what is equally important, with one another by air routes, the network of communications thus created will not only confer air power, it will also consolidate the Empire and give a unity to widely scattered peoples unattainable hitherto."†

With the increasing range and mobility of aircraft and the formation of a chain of bases throughout the long lines of our communications, we shall be able so to dispose our air forces as to meet most effectively the changing conditions. In this disposition it is imperative that the Dominion air forces shall co-operate in peace as in war, for this alone will tend to ensure instant preparedness to meet an attack.

One of the resolutions recorded at the Imperial Conference, 1923, was the following :—

" The necessity for the maintenance by Great Britain of a Home Defence Air Force of sufficient strength to give adequate protection against air attack by the strongest air force within striking distance of her shores."

The economic and geographical conditions which emphasize the necessity for this may be stated as :— (1) Great density of population; (2) Dependence upon supplies from overseas; and (3) Proximity to Continental powers.

* Sir Samuel Hoare in a speech in London on " Some Aspects of Imperial Defence."
† Lord Thomson on "Air and Empire."—*Observer*, Oct. 24th, 1926.

The striking force of Great Britain has hitherto rested upon the sea. Our superiority there is just as important now as in the past for the maintenance of our communications and trade, and for the transport of our armies across the sea; yet it relies to an increasing extent upon our superiority in the air. The vulnerability of Great Britain to air attack is greater than that of its Continental neighbours. The protection which it has been afforded in the past by its insularity no longer exists.

The military policy of Great Britain in Europe has been the maintenance of the balance of power. Her strategic position has frequently bestowed upon her in the past the position of umpire, a rôle which she can scarcely hope to occupy in these days of developing air power. The control of the resources and manufacturing efficiency of Western and Central Europe by any one Continental power would enable it to outbuild our Navy and obtain mastery of the sea, and would preclude the establishment of our bases in any Continental war on the coast of an allied state, as has been our custom.

Again, the area just indicated provides a field most favourable to the action of nations in alliance, for in this case operations in the air are more advantageous than those on sea or land, as there are not the geographical obstructions which impede the action of allied armies, nor the tactical difficulties inherent to a combined army or fleet.

It follows, then, that Great Britain, which is particularly vulnerable to air attack, is also especially exposed to it, and such an attack involves much less risk to European nations than naval blockade and military invasion. Adequate protection against such an attack is therefore of vital importance to Great Britain.

In South Africa the problem is one of defensive operations chiefly over land, and as such we may expect to see her land aircraft developed with little consideration for operations over the sea. Here, then, national defence can best be secured in the future by the possession of an efficient air force capable of dealing with any eventuality. Such air force will also be an acquisition in maintaining law and order throughout the country and in dealing with any internal disorders amongst the native population. A strong air force will reduce the necessity for keeping an unduly large army and will be employed more economically and effectively. The scope for civil aviation throughout the Dominions is a great asset, and once this is commonly established it will prove invaluable in the development and the defence of those countries.

In the case of Canada, national defence against air attack must, on account of the extensive line of her land frontier, be one of the most difficult problems with which any of our Dominions will be confronted. We are, however, happy in the thought that the peoples bounding her frontier are linked together with ties of blood and common policy.

The measures necessary for the defence of the Empire are almost insupportable if left entirely to the Mother Country. Nevertheless, we cannot afford to neglect them, for they are vital to our existence.

"The very foundations of Imperial defence policy must be first, unity of organisation among and control over the forces of the Empire, and then the assurance of free inter-communication between its various portions, for without this, mutual co-operation and support are impossible."*

To the Empire no question is of greater importance than security from the possible attack of its scattered units; their defence must depend in the last issue on the strength and efficiency of the fighting forces, here and in the Dominions. The peculiar geographical composition of the Empire, and the long stretches of sea communications throughout the world renders its defence radically different from those confronting other nations. The reports issued at the Imperial Conference

*The Direction of War. W. D. Bird.

of 1926 are encouraging and show quite clearly that each Dominion is alive to its own responsibility in the matter of Imperial defence as a whole. One main point which is steadily kept in view is the necessity for co-ordination in the training and organization of Dominion forces of every kind on the same lines as those pursued by the naval, military, and air force authorities of Great Britain. To quote Mr. Bruce, the Prime Minister of Australia, this uniformity in organization, methods of training, equipment, etc., ensures that in time of emergency each of the Empire's forces may dovetail into any formation with which those forces may be needed to co-operate.

A nation possessing efficient air forces is enabled not only to defend its interests in the air, but also to aid the sea and land operations effectively. The following may be said to be the most important factors that decide the strategy of these forces :—

(a) A powerful and efficient force, sufficient in strength to ensure air superiority, to guarantee the safety of our country and Empire from air attack, and to support naval and military operations.

(b) Properly equipped air bases so situated that the units occupying those bases are able to use their offensive powers to the utmost over those areas where hostilities are expected, in addition to supplying the necessary local defence.

(c) A prosperous aircraft industry based on a world-wide civil aviation, due to the creation of air routes, linking up the Dominions with the Mother Country.

With a view to readiness for immediate action in any part of the world, it is necessary for the strategist in peace time to study distribution and relative strength. He must think "Imperially," and not of the single purpose of home defence. Plans must be discussed, co-ordinated and adopted by the respective governments of our Dominions, and these must be constantly reviewed with the development of flying.

In presenting the Air Estimates for 1926-27, the Secretary of State for Air (Sir Samuel Hoare) outlined our air policy, the main points of which were as follows:—

Our policy must

(1) Provide for home defence against air attack.

(2) It must provide for air defence in such parts of the Empire as are suited to it.

(3) It must undertake the required air work for the Navy and Army.

(4) It must develop civil air routes over the face of the Empire, and generally extend the knowledge and practice of the air among all classes of the community.

These four principles were dealt with at some length. With regard to home defence: "The first duty of the Air Service and by far the most important was to provide for the defence of these shores against possible air attack. To-day we were in the position of being the second greatest air power in the world. Even so, we were still in an inferiority of somewhat less than one to two as compared with the total strength of our nearest neighbour."

With regard to the fourth principle—"The development of civil aviation generally"—the Secretary of State said that "the Air Ministry attaches enormous importance to the policy of developing Empire air communications, and regards it *as one of the basic foundations of any national air policy*. The organization of Empire air routes affects both military and civil flying. Obviously, if a system of air communications can be developed over the Empire, it will make it easier to develop *a more mobile Empire defence*.

"The last principal object of a national air policy is," he said, "the creation of an instructed public opinion on air questions, the expansion of air knowledge and air practice in a much wider circle than at present exists. It was with this main object in view that the

Auxiliary and Special Reserve squadrons have been created."

Continuing, the Air Minister said that " it might be the case, that, however efficient our Air Force was, it could never make it impossible for an attacking force to penetrate these shores, but he was sure that, provided their expansion programme was carried out, *and that they had an Air Force of the size contemplated,* they might look forward to making it very risky for a foreign power to attack this country." In other words, there can be no victory for either side *without fighting for it,* and it follows from this that the *chief rôle of the air forces* must, in the first instance, lie in the defeat of the enemy's air forces. Until these have been overcome, and " air superiority " attained, *successful* air operations such as bombing attacks cannot be undertaken. Provided our defence is sound, that is, that we possess sufficient fighters and an efficient anti-aircraft and searchlight barrage, enemy bombing craft in the face of such opposition will be open to defeat or will be prevented from attaining their object.

Air warfare, like sea or land warfare, is but a means towards an end. The primary aim of an air force is to gain or maintain air superiority—that is, liberty of movement and action in the air—consequently, its object is to clear the air of hostile aircraft, and until this has been gained, an air force cannot operate without grave risk.

In his book, " The Reformation of War," Col. Fuller writes : " Though it is a truism to state that the basic factor in war is man, it is not generally recognised that whether man fights on the land or on the sea or in the air the elements of war are the same, namely, moral, weapons, movement and protection ; consequently whatever mode of war is to be examined, in these elements we find a common denominator to all those forces. If this be accepted as correct, then I see no reason why warfare as a whole should not be treated as *one* subject." The more one studies war in all elements, the more I think one realizes the soundness of this. Continuing, the same writer expresses as his personal opinion—an opinion which, I think, will be shared by the majority of those who have studied war in all its elements—" that the principles of war, *e.g.*,

"(1) The Principle of the Objective,
"(2) ,, ,, ,, ,, Offensive,
"(3) ,, ,, ,, ,, Security,
"(4) ,, ,, ,, ,, Concentration,
"(5) ,, ,, ,, ,, Economy of Force,
"(6) ,, ,, ,, ,, Movement,
"(7) ,, ,, ,, ,, Surprise,
"(8) ,, ,, ,, ,, Co-operation,

are as applicable to sea and to air warfare as to land warfare, irrespective of the differences in the three spheres of action in which these three modes of warfare take place, the spheres of sea, air and land. The ultimate objective is the same, namely, the maintenance of policy. The two great means are the same—offensive and defensive action, whether material, physical or moral. The methods of potentiating these are identical —concentration and economy, movement and surprise, and the ultimate co-ordination is the same—co-operation within fleets, armies and air forces and co-operation between them as parts of one single defence force. It is this co-operation which, I consider, forms the foundation of grand tactics, not as heretofore interpreted—the major battle plan of an army, or of a navy, or of an air force, but of an army, a navy and an air force intimately co-operating in order to attain a common objective— the maintenance of policy.

"In an army, navy or air force individually, security of hitting demands a close co-operation of all arms in order to attain the grand tactical objective—the destruction of the enemy's fighting strength. When these forces are combined in one plan, then, to the above co-operation must be added a mutual co-operation between the three themselves. This co-operation, whether within one force or between two or three forces, is virtually the execution of the grand tactical plan of battle or campaign; and it is important to remember that a plan is as necessary for a campaign as for a battle, and that, consequently, every battle plan must form an economic part of the general plan of campaign."

The author explains that in this plan there are four grand tactical acts which may be carried out, either separately or in combination, namely, surprise, attrition, envelopment and penetration. "Visibly," he says, "these acts are equally applicable to all modes of warfare—sea, land or air, and whether made use of separately or combined, these acts constitute the common denominator of the plan or idea of campaign.

"The setting in motion of this plan is usually called strategy, that is the secure movement of troops to that point of decision at which it is hoped to defeat the enemy. In the past, in spite of the universal nature of the principles of war, there has been a land strategy, a sea strategy, and the future may possibly see added to these two, an air strategy. This process of separating strategy into three compartments I believe to be fundamentally uneconomical and a direct violation of the principle of economy of forces as applied to a united army, navy and air force, and hence a weakening of the principle of the objective."

I hope that the contents of this book support this view, and in addition will be found in keeping with the policy advocated by the present Air Minister, Sir Samuel Hoare, who, in the course of his speech on the 1926-27 Air Estimates, is reported as saying: "So far as his advisers and he were concerned, they would do everything in their power to make that co-operation as close as they could and *to apply their policy in such a way as to bring the greatest possible unity of outlook between the three Services as a whole.*"

To achieve this end, we must ever remember that the other services have their point of view, and it is for us to endeavour to reconcile it with our own.

" Principles of war, though they can be simply stated, are not easy to learn, and can never be learned from books alone. They are the principles of human nature; and whoever learned from books how to deal successfully with his fellows? War which drives human nature to its last resources is a great engine of education, teaching no lessons which it does not illustrate, and enforcing all its lessons by bitter penalties. The most that a book can do is to quicken perception and prepare the mind for the teaching of experience."*

War in the Air. Raleigh.

Parts I and II of Mr. Winston Churchill's remarkable work, " The World Crisis, 1916-1918," have appeared on the eve of this book being published.

Appendix V, Part II, of " The World Crisis " contains a Memorandum written on October 21st, 1917, by Mr. Winston Churchill. This memorandum is of such considerable interest to the subject matter of this book that I have thought fit to include it. The opinions expressed in this memorandum will, I think, be found to possess much in common with many of the principles founded in the chapters of this book. I would draw my readers' attention in particular to the passages of this memorandum I have caused to be printed in *italics*.

The memorandum in question will be found in the Appendices.

K

APPENDICES.

APPENDIX I.

*MEMORANDUM BY Mr. WINSTON CHURCHILL OF OCTOBER 21ST, 1917.

Most important of all the mechanical factors which are available, comes the Air Offensive. So much progress in thought has been made on this subject, even since this paper was under preparation, that it is not necessary to dwell upon it at any length. But there are certain general principles which may be stated or re-stated.

War proceeds by slaughter and manœuvre. Manœuvre consists either in operations of Surprise or in operations against the flanks and communications of the enemy. Owing to the lines now stretching continuously from the Alps to the sea, there are no flanks. But the Germans, striking under the sea at our vital communications, have threatened us with a decisive peril, which we are warding off only by an immense diversion of our resources. If we take on the one hand the amount of national life-energy which the Germans have put into their submarine attack, and compare it with the amount of national life-energy we are compelled to devote to meeting and overcoming that attack, it will be apparent what a fearfully profitable operation this attack on our communications has been to the enemy. Would it be an exaggeration to say that for one war-power unit Germany has applied to the submarine attack we have been forced to assign fifteen or twenty?

Even better than an operation against communications is an operation against bases. Air predominance affords the possibility of striking at both. It can either paralyse the enemy's military action, or compel him to devote to the defence of his bases and communications a share of his straitened resources far greater than what we need in the attack.

* Appendix V, Part II, " The World Crisis, 1916-1918," by the Rt. Hon. Winston S. Churchill, C.H., M.P.

All attacks on communications or bases should have their relation to the main battle. It is not reasonable to speak of an air offensive as if it were going to finish the war by itself. It is improbable that any terrorization of the civil population which could be achieved by air attack would compel the Government of a great nation to surrender. Familiarity with bombardment, a good system of dug-outs or shelters, a strong control by police and military authorities, should be sufficient to preserve the national fighting power unimpaired. In our own case we have seen the combative spirit of the people roused, and not quelled, by the German air raids. Nothing that we have learned of the capacity of the German population to endure suffering justifies us in assuming that they could be cowed into submission by such methods, or indeed that they would not be rendered more desperately resolved by them. *Therefore our air offensive should consistently be directed at striking at the bases and communications upon whose structure the fighting power of the enemy's armies and his fleets of the sea and of the air depends.* Any injury which comes to the civil population from this process of attack must be regarded as incidental and inevitable.

The supreme and direct object of an air offensive is to deprive the German armies on the Western Front of their capacity for resistance. It must therefore be applied and reach its maximum development in proper relation to the main battles both of Exhaustion and Surprise during the culminating period of our general offensive. German armies whose communications were continually impeded and interrupted and whose bases were unceasingly harried might still, in spite of all that could be done from the air, be able to maintain themselves in the field and keep the front. But if at the same time that this great difficulty and menace to their services in rear had reached its maximum, they were also subjected to the intense strain of a great offensive on the ground proceeding by battles both of Exhaustion and Surprise, the complete defeat and breaking up of their armies in the West as a whole might not perhaps be beyond the bounds of possibility. There is an immense difference between merely keeping an army fed and supplied on a comparatively quiescent front in spite of air attacks, and resisting the kind of offensive which the British are delivering at the present time. It is imperative that the defending army should be able to move hundreds of thousands of tons of stores and ammunition within very limited times to the battle-front, and to maintain a most rapid circulation of hundreds of thousands of troops; and the double strain of doing this under a really overwhelming air attack might well prove fatal. More especially might this be hoped for if the form of our offensive were not confined simply to the main battle-front, but if it were so varied in locality and direction as to require from the enemy *an exceptional degree of lateral mobility. For our air offensive to attain its full effect, it is necessary that our ground offensive should be of a character to throw the greatest possible strain upon the enemy's communications.*

We have greatly suffered and are still suffering in the progress of our means of air warfare from the absence of a proper General Staff studying the possibilities of air warfare, not merely as an ancillary service to the special operations of the Army or the Navy, but also as an independent arm co-operating in the general plan. *Material developments must necessarily be misguided so long as they do not relate to a definite War Plan for the Air, which again is combined with the general War Plan.*

In consequence of this, many very important points are still in doubt or in dispute on which systematized Staff study could have by now given clear pronouncements. The dominating and immediate interests of the army and the navy have overlaid air warfare, and prevented many promising lines of investigation from being pursued with the necessary science and authority. Extreme diversities of opinion prevail as to the degree of effectiveness which can be expected from aerial attack. It is disputed whether air attack can ever really shatter communications, bases, or aerodromes. It is contended that aerodromes are difficult to discover and still more difficult to hit; that tons of bombs have been discharged on particular aerodromes without denying their use to the enemy; that railway junctions and communications have been repeatedly bombed without preventing appreciably the immense and continuous movement of men and material necessary to the fighting armies; that no bombardment from the air, especially at great distances from our own lines, can compare in intensity with the kind of bombardment from artillery, in spite of which, nevertheless, operations of a military and even semi-military character are continuously carried on.

On the other hand, it is claimed that aerial warfare has never yet been practised except in miniature; that bombing in particular has never been studied as a science; that the hitting of objectives from great heights by day or night is worthy of as intense a volume of scientific study as, for instance, is brought to bear upon perfecting the gunnery of the Fleet; that much of the unfavourable data accumulated showing the comparative ineffectiveness of bombing consists of results of unscientific action—for instance, dropping bombs singly without proper sighting apparatus or specially trained " bomb droppers " (the equivalent of " gun layers "), instead of dropping them in regulated salvos by specially trained men, so as to " straddle " the targets properly. It is believed by the sanguine school that a very high degree of accuracy, similar to that which has been attained at sea under extraordinarily difficult circumstances, could be achieved if something like the same scientific knowledge and intense determination were brought to bear.

Secondly, it is pointed out that an air offensive has never been considered on the same scale or with the same ruthlessness in regard to losses for adequate objects as prevail in the operations of armies. Aeroplanes have never been used to attack vital objectives in the same spirit as infantry have been used, viz., regardless of loss, the attack being repeated again and again until the objective is secured. It is pointed out that in 1918 numbers will for the first time become available for operations, not merely on the larger scale, but of a totally different character.

On the assumption that these more sanguine views are justly founded, the primary objective of our air forces becomes plainly apparent, viz., the air bases of the enemy and the consequent destruction of his air fighting forces. All other objectives, however tempting, however necessary it may be to make provision for attacking some of them, must be regarded as subordinate to this primary purpose. If for instance our numerical superiority in the air were sufficient at a certain period next year to enable us in the space of two or three weeks to locate and destroy by bomb and fire, either from a great height or if necessary from quite low down, all or nearly all the enemy's hangars, and make unusable all or nearly all his landing grounds and starting grounds within 50 or 60 miles of his front line, his air forces might be definitely beaten, and once beaten could be kept beaten.

Once this result was achieved and real mastery of the air obtained, all sorts of enterprises which are now not possible would become easy. All kinds of aeroplanes which it is not now possible to use on the fighting fronts could come into play. Considerable parties of soldiers could be conveyed by air to the neighbourhood of bridges or other important points, and, having overwhelmed the local guard could *from the ground* effect a regular and permanent demolition. The destruction of particular important factories could also be achieved by carefully organized expeditions of this kind. " Flying columns " (literally) of this character could be organized to operate far and wide in the enemy's territory, thus forcing him to disperse in an indefinite defensive good troops urgently needed at the front. All his camps, depots, etc., could be made the object of constant organized machine-gun attack from low-flying squadrons. *But the indispensable preliminary to all results in the air, as in every other sphere of war, is to defeat the armed forces of the enemy.*

APPENDIX II

IMPERIAL CONFERENCE, 1926.

The conclusions reached by the Imperial Conference on the subject of defence may be summarized as follow: —

1. The Resolutions on Defence adopted at the last session of the Conference are reaffirmed.

"(a) The Conference affirms that it is necessary to provide for the adequate defence of the territories and trade of the several countries comprising the British Empire.

"(b) In this connection the Conference expressly recognizes that it is for the Parliaments of the several parts of the Empire, upon recommendations of their respective Governments, to decide the nature and extent of any action which should be taken by them.

"(c) Subject to this provision the Conference suggests the following guiding principles: —

"(i) The primary responsibility for each portion of the Empire represented at the Conference for its own local defence.

"(ii) Adequate provision for safeguarding the maritime communications of the several parts of the Empire and the routes and waterways along and through which their armed forces and trade pass.

"(iii) The provision of naval bases and facilities for repair and fuel so as to ensure the mobility of the fleets.

"(iv) The desirability of the maintenance of a minimum standard of naval strength—namely, equality with the naval strength of any foreign Power in accordance with the provisions of the Washington Treaty on Limitation of Armaments as approved by Great Britain, all the self-governing Dominions, and India.

"(v) The desirability of the development of the air forces in the several countries of the Empire upon such lines as will make it possible, by means of the adoption, as far as practical, of a common system of organization and training and the use of uniform manuals, patterns of arms, equipment, and stores (with the exception of the type of aircraft), for each part of the Empire as it may determine to co-operate with other parts with the least possible delay and the greatest efficiency.

"(d) In the application of these principles to the several parts of the Empire concerned the Conference takes note of:—

"(i) The deep interest of the Commonwealth of Australia, the Dominion of New Zealand, and India, in the provision of a naval base at Singapore as essential for ensuring the mobility necessary to provide for the securing of the territories and trade of the Empire in Eastern waters;

"(ii) The necessity for the maintenance of safe passage along the great route to the East through the Mediterranean and the Red Sea;

"(iii) The necessity for the maintenance by Great Britain of a Home Defence Air Force of sufficient strength to give adequate protection against air attack by the strongest air force within striking distance of her shores.

"(e) The Conference, while deeply concerned for the paramount importance of providing for the safety and integrity of all parts of the Empire, earnestly desires, so far as is consistent with this consideration, the further limitation of armaments, and trusts that no opportunity may be lost to promote this object."

2. The Imperial Conference regrets that it has not been possible to make greater progress with the international reduction and limitation of armaments referred to in these Resolutions. It is the common desire of the Governments represented at this Conference to do their utmost in pursuit of this object so far as this is consistent with the safety and integrity of all parts of the Empire and its communications.

3. The Conference recognizes that, even after a large measure of reduction and limitation of armaments has been achieved, a considerable effort will be involved in order to maintain the minimum standard of naval strength contemplated in the Washington Treaty on Limitation of

Armaments—namely, equality with the naval strength of any foreign Power. It has noted the statements set forth by the Admiralty as to the formidable expenditure required within coming years for the replacement of warships, as they become obsolete, by up-to-date ships.

4. Impressed with the vital importance of ensuring the security of the world-wide trade routes upon which the safety and welfare of all parts of the Empire depend, the representatives of Australia, New Zealand, and India note with special interest the steps already taken by His Majesty's Government in Great Britain to develop the Naval Base at Singapore, with the object of facilitating the free movement of the Fleets. In view of the heavy expenditure involved, they welcome the spirit of co-operation shown in the contributions made with the object of expediting this work.

5. The Conference observes that steady progress has been made in the direction of organizing military formations in general on similar lines; in the adoption of similar patterns of weapons; and in the interchange of officers between different parts of the Empire; it invites the Governments concerned to consider the possibility of extending these forms of co-operation and of promoting further consultation between the respective General Staffs on defence questions adjudged of common interest.

6. (a) The Conference takes note with satisfaction of the substantial progress that has been made since 1923 in building up the air forces and resources of the several parts of the Empire.

(b) Recognizing that the fullest mobility is essential to the effective and economical employment of air power, the Conference recommends, for the consideration of the several Governments, the adoption of the following principle:—The necessity for creating and maintaining an adequate chain of air bases and refuelling stations.

(c) Impressed with the desirability of still closer co-ordination in this as in all other spheres of common interest, and in particular with the advantages which should follow from a more general dissemination of the experience acquired in the use of this new arm under the widely varying conditions which obtain in different parts of the Empire, the Conference recommends for consideration by Governments interested the adoption in principle of a system of mutual interchange of individual officers for liaison and other duties, and of complete air units, so far as local requirements and resources permit.

7. The Conference recognizes that the defence of India already throws upon the Government of India responsibilities of a specially onerous character, and takes note of their decision to create a Royal Indian Navy.

8. The Conference notes with satisfaction that considerable progress in the direction of closer co-operation in defence matters has been effected by the reciprocal attachment of naval, military, and air officers to the Staff Colleges and other technical establishments maintained in various parts of the Empire, and invites the attention of the Governments represented to the facilities afforded by the New Imperial Defence College in London for the education of officers in the broadest aspects of strategy.

9. The Conference takes note of the developments in the organization of the Committee of Imperial Defence since the session of 1923. It invites the attention of the Governments represented at the Conference to the following resolutions adopted with a view to consultation in questions of common defence at a meeting of the Committee of Imperial Defence held on May 30th, 1911, in connection with the Imperial Conference of that year:

" i. That one or more representatives appointed by the respective Governments of the Dominions should be invited to attend meetings of the Committee of Imperial defence when questions of naval and military (the words ' and air ' would be required to bring the resolution up to date) defence affecting the overseas Dominions are under consideration.

" ii. The proposal that a Defence Committee should be established in each Dominion is accepted in principle. The constitution of these Defence Committees is a matter for each Dominion to decide."

APPENDIX III.

THE COMMITTEE OF IMPERIAL DEFENCE.

"*Carendo Tutus.*"
(Safe by taking precautions.)

The following are extracts from the speech on the subject of Imperial Defence made by Mr. Baldwin at the meeting of the Imperial Conference, 1926:—

(1) The C.I.D. is our principal organ for the co-ordination of all activities in the sphere of defence. It is emphasized that this Committee is purely *advisory and consultative* in character.

(2) The Committee consists of the Prime Minister and any person whom he chooses to invite to attend. This elasticity of organization proves of the greatest value and is made use of extensively, particularly in the case of sub-committees to which questions are referred for detailed examination and report.

It is necessary to realize that modern war is no longer a matter solely of navies, armies and air forces of professional sailors, soldiers and airmen, but one in which all the resources of a nation may have to become engaged. The great network of committees is based on its recognition.

(3) Broadly speaking, the work divides itself into two main branches concerned with the co-ordination of the fighting services and the ancillary work of the civilian departments respectively.

The whole work is co-ordinated by the C.I.D., with the assistance of a permanent secretariat.

C.I.D.		
Committee of CHIEFS OF STAFF.	MAN POWER Committee.	PRINCIPAL SUPPLY Officers Committee.

(4) CHIEFS OF STAFF COMMITTEE.—In addition to his function as adviser on sea, land or air policy, as the case may be, the Chief of Staff of each service has an individual and collective responsibility, as a member of this Committee, for advising on defence policy as a whole. The C.I.D. is thus enabled to receive *collective advice* instead of separate and possibly contradictory advice from the three angles of sea, land and air warfare.

(5) MAN POWER COMMITTEE.—Deals with the organization of our man power in time of war.

(6) PRINCIPAL SUPPLY OFFICERS COMMITTEE.—Fills in the field of Supply, an advisory and co-ordinating function similar to that of the Chiefs of Staff Committee in Staff questions.

(7) As part of the general policy of improving the methods of communication and consultation on matters of interest common to all sections of the Empire, the Dominions are asked to consider how far they can, in the interest of co-ordination of defence, make further use of the elastic machinery of the C.I.D. More frequent association and closer co-operation with the work of the Committee on all matters affecting the Dominions or the general defence of the Empire is welcomed.

(8) IMPERIAL DEFENCE COLLEGE.—The function of the College is to train a body of officers, and eventually, perhaps, of civilian officials, in the broadest aspects of Imperial strategy, and the occasional examination of current problems of Imperial Defence referred to it by the Chiefs of Staff Committee, in which the supervision of the College for professional purposes will be vested. It is hoped that the College will provide a considerable stimulus to the further promotion of team-work between the Services.

www.ingramcontent.com/pod-product-compliance
Lightning Source LLC
Chambersburg PA
CBHW070851050426
42453CB00012B/2138